Dedication

To our mothers, grandmothers, great-grandmothers and all the women who contributed so mightily to the settling and taming of this raw land called "The West," and who along the way managed to make the whole experience taste pretty darn good.

–DAVID A. POULSEN, BARB POULSEN, LAUREN HITCHNER

The Cowboy Country Cookbook

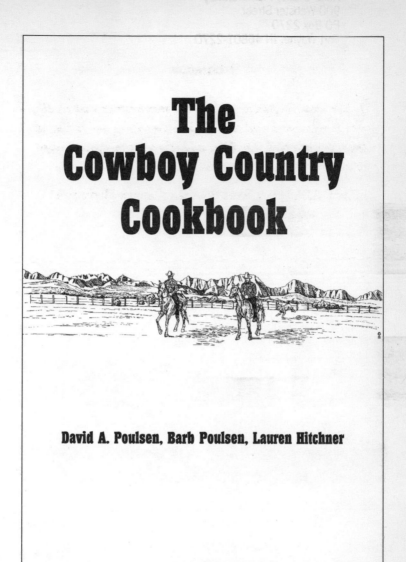

David A. Poulsen, Barb Poulsen, Lauren Hitchner

Roundup
BOOKS
Red Deer College Press

The Publishers
Red Deer College Press
56 Avenue & 32 Street Box 5005
Red Deer Alberta Canada T4N 5H5

Acknowledgments
Edited for the Press by Patricia Couture.
Designed by Dennis Johnson.
Cover illustration by Jeff Hitch.
Half-title page illustration by John Duffy.
Special thanks to Boldface Technologies.
Printed and bound in Canada by Webcom Limited
for Red Deer College Press.

Financial support provided by the Alberta Foundation for the Arts, a beneficiary of the Lottery Fund of the Government of Alberta, the Department of Canadian Heritage and Red Deer College.

COMMITTED TO THE DEVELOPMENT OF CULTURE AND THE ARTS

5 4 3 2 1

Canadian Cataloguing in Publication Data
Poulsen, David A., 1946–
The cowboy country cookbook

(Roundup books)
ISBN 0-88995-162-4

1. Cookery, American—Western style. I. Poulsen, Barb, 1958–
II. Hitchner, Lauren, 1946– III. Title. IV. Series: Roundup books
(Red Deer, Alta)
TX715.2.W47P68   1997   641.5978   C96-910774-9

The following recipes are used by permission:

The Wolf Trapper's Cookbook by Nan McHalek Creek
Chicken-Fried Steak
Cedar Creek Catfish Fry
Pecan Pie

Best Little Cookbook in the West by Jean Hoare
Jean's Beans, at Home or in Camp
Beef Wellington
Roasted Baron of Beef
Buffalo Ribs
Chicken-in-the-Gold
Prince of Wales Cake

Contents

Contributors' Brands

Introduction

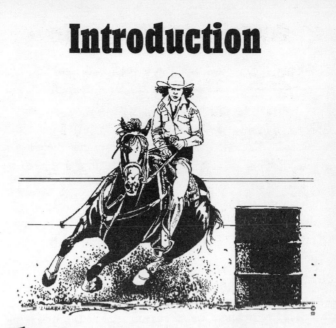

AS LONG AS THERE HAVE BEEN CATTLE AND PEOPLE whose job it is to tend them, other people have been fascinated by the relationship between the two. In particular, the movement of cattle from place to place has captured the imaginations of observers. Throughout history, writers, artists and, more recently, filmmakers have painstakingly sought to record the drama of the cattle drive and the daring feats of stockmen as they moved herds to markets or distant grazing grounds.

While many of us might credit dime novels or the brushes of Charlie Russell and Frederic Remington with first depicting life as it revolved around the world of cattle, the story is, in fact, a much older one. *The Book of Genesis* tells us that the patriarch Abraham, finding the ranges of the Ur of the Chaldees too crowded for his liking, drove his herd west to the land of Canaan. So while Abraham may not have spent much time in the saddle, he certainly qualifies as one of the earliest cowboys.

We find the first mention of the word *cowboy* not in Owen Wister's *The Virginian*, which is considered by most scholars to be the first western novel, but in Irish writings of about 1000 A.D. The English then borrowed the term and brought it to America, where it was given a new meaning though not precisely the one we associate with the word today. The earliest North American use of the word *cowboy* referred to the rough adventurers of the newly formed Republic of Texas who in the 1830s made a practice of raiding the Mexican ranges and driving stolen cattle back north. Yep, the first cowboys were rustlers. But even they had their predecessors—witness Sir Walter Scott's accounts of the cattle stealing borderers in *Rob Roy*.

It was Christopher Columbus who introduced cattle to the New World. On his second voyage in 1497, the Spanish explorer brought both horses and "beeves" to the island of Santa Domingo. Twenty-nine years later, Gregoria de Villalobos transported cattle from Santa Domingo to Mexico, and from that time on, wherever Spanish explorers and missionaries went, they took livestock with them. For example, when Coronado struck out in search of the Seven Cities of Cibolla in 1540, he took along sheep, goats, hogs and five hundred head of cattle.

The northward movement of Spaniards and cattle continued, and in 1748 Jose de Escanados brought the first stock to the fertile Nueces and Rio Grande valleys of Texas. The herds grew and, as fenced ranchland had yet to take shape, the cattle were left to run free under the watchful eye of the missionary-trained *vaqueros* (meaning "mounted workers with cows"). These magnificent horsemen were to have a profound influence on the evolution of the cowboy to the north. In fact, the American cowboy is indebted to his Spanish ancestor for everything from the equipment of his trade to much of the language we associate with his life. Words like *stampede, lariat* and *chaps* are all Spanish in origin, and even *vaquero* itself has been Anglicized to become *buckaroo*.

Less than a century after the first cattle arrived in Texas, they outnumbered two-legged Texans by six to one. And the look of the cattle began to change. While the roots of the Texas cattle industry and the cattle themselves were Spanish, the arrival of Stephen Austin and his colonists from the east brought an Anglo-American influence. For one thing, the settlers brought with them descendants of the fleshier English Longhorn cattle. These, when crossed with wild cattle already in Texas, produced the Texas longhorn, the lean, lanky animal with a deadly spread of horns that could sometimes measure as much as six feet across. The Texas longhorn was to become as much a pioneer in the developing American West as the men and women who carved out homesteads in the frontier wilderness.

While there was some movement of cattle northward before and during the Civil War, the real migration came in the years immediately after. By then, Texas was teeming with cattle (as many as one quarter of them running free and unbranded), and young Texans returning home from the war saw cattle as their one economic asset. The industrialized east wanted beef (in New York City the price of sirloin steak was an astronomical twenty-five to thirty cents a pound), there were surrendered Indians and Midwest miners to feed and, farther north, lush new grazing ranges to stock.

Texans seized the opportunity. What followed was a massive roundup and movement northward that over the next twenty years would involve millions of head of Texas longhorn cattle. But first there were difficulties to overcome. The first attempts to move herds to railheads in Missouri and Kansas were beset with problems. In the first place, the residents of those states wanted nothing to do with longhorn cattle or the fractious men who accompanied them. This wasn't simply stubborn intransigence or carried-over animosity from Civil War days though both probably played their part. More importantly, the longhorns carried with them ticks that spread the deadly tick fever. Immune to the disease themselves, the longhorns were sure death to Northern cattle that so much as crossed a longhorn trail.

And there were obstacles during the drives themselves. Indians, while peaceable for the most part, often demanded a toll for the grass consumed by the cattle. More dangerous were the Kansas Jayhawkers, settler-outlaws who had sympathized with the North and had little use for what they regarded as Southern trespassers. The Jayhawkers, too, demanded compensation, but violence was often the outcome. Adding to the man-made hardships were those provided by Mother Nature. Mud, floods, storms and grass-killing frost were constant threats to the longhorn cattle whose skitishness made them especially susceptible to stampedes. All of this resulted in trail losses that threatened to end the migration north before it had really begun.

In fact, the drives might have ceased altogether had it not been for an enterprising Yankee stockman and cattle buyer named Joseph McCoy, who sought to establish a cattle shipping center that would make it possible for Texas cattle to supply the eastern demand for beef. McCoy settled on the tiny hamlet of Abilene, Kansas, situated near the western end of the Kansas Pacific rail line. He built stockyards and a hotel and in 1867 transported thirty-five thousand head of longhorns east. By 1871 the number of cattle being shipped had swelled to an astonishing seven hundred thousand.

As critical as Abilene was to the cattle boom, the routes used to get the beef from Texas to Kansas were just as important, and none was more significant than the Chisholm Trail. Named after Jesse Chisholm, who a few years earlier had used a one-time buffalo route to haul his supply wagons to buyers along the way, it quickly became the most popular pathway between Texas and Kansas. After the establishment of Abilene as a railhead, so many cattle would tread those miles that, years after the Chisholm Trail had ceased to be used, a depression the width of four football fields still marked the famous route. As the railroad extended west, new shipping points sprung up: Ellsworth, Wichita and finally Dodge, the most famous of the trail towns.

Of course, not all of the cattle went east in rail cars. Following the lead of Charles Goodnight and Oliver Loving, who established a prosperous ranch in Colorado (their story in part inspired Larry McMurtry's *Lonesome Dove*), Texas cattlemen drove herds north to the open ranges of Colorado, Wyoming, Montana and Nebraska and eventually to the western provinces of Canada.

Spectacular though the movement of the cattle was, it was as short-lived as it was dramatic. Farmers, sheepmen and small-scale ranchers arrived on the scene, which resulted in often violent confrontations with the cattle barons. Barbed wire was introduced and used to close off the open range. And then came the devasting winter of 1886–87, which killed cattle in the thousands. By 1890 the movement of cattle northward slowed to a trickle and the days of the freelance cowboy came to an end along with the era of the open range. Never again would thousands of cattle roam endless free range. The West of the twentieth century was already being established. Fenced pastures, cultivated fields and cowboys who were most often ranch employees were the new order.

To the north, the cattle kingdom chapter of Canadian history began rather differently, although it concluded in much the same way. It was authored initially by the men in scarlet: the North-West Mounted Police. Dispatched west to rein in the lawlessness of the American whiskey traders and to quell the unrest of an Indian nation unhappy with the systematic elimination of the buffalo, the Mounties were important to the development of the West in general and to the birth of the cattle industry in particular.

The Mounted Police gave security to newly established beef producers and provided a small but steady market for beef. Demand increased as Canadian Pacific Railway contractors pushed west and the Department of the Interior established Indian food requirements. For a time, before the arrival of the large cattle companies, retired members of the police force formed a vital part of the ranch community.

Calgary, nestled in the heart of the grass-rich foothills, got an early start toward becoming the capital of the Canadian cattle kingdom when Methodist missionary John McDougall brought a small herd on a fifty-six-day drive from Fort Garry to his father's newly established mission at nearby Morley on the Bow River. In 1875 John Shaw brought a large herd of nearly 450 head to the region from the interior of British Columbia, where a thriving cattle industry had been serving the needs of miners for a decade. Meanwhile, cheap leaseland made the prairies particularly attractive to speculating stockmen, and giant ranches like the Cochrane, Bar U, Oxley and Waldron were established.

One man whose contribution stands out for the sheer volume of cattle he brought into Canada was Tom Lynch. After driving and selling several herds, he and partner George Emerson decided the grass beside the Highwood River would be an ideal place to establish a ranch. They assembled a herd of one thousand head in Miles City, Montana, and drove them north into Canada. Eventually, the partnership was dissolved with Emerson heading farther west into the hills, while Lynch settled on the south side of the Highwood and established the famous TL.

To the east, what was to become Saskatchewan was keeping pace with giant spreads of its own appearing in the Cypress Hills, among them the 76, the Hitchcock and the Matador. On the other side of the Rockies, ranches large and small were springing up in the Nicola, Caricoo and Chilcotin districts. The Douglas Lake, the Gang and the Empire Valley ranches were among the most prominent.

For a time the Canadian cattle industry rivaled that of its neighbor to the south, but it would soon face many of the same problems. A government-sponsored settlement program brought hundreds of newcomers armed with barbed wire, which was one of the greatest threats to the open range. Sheepmen came, too, and so did summer droughts and winter blizzards. Soon the Canadian cattle industry found itself in decline.

Eventually, as had already happened in the United States, the Canadian West was inundated with people whose interests came in conflict with those of the cattle producers. And, as was the case on the southern free ranges, those of the north were to disappear or at least be dramatically altered in the face of this onslaught.

The twenty-five years during which the cattle kingdom was

born and flourished was a time of danger and daring and of people whose exploits (some real, some imagined) continue to captivate the imaginations of writers, artists and filmmakers more than a century later. The cowboy is still the most imitated figure in our society. The chisel-faced, freedom-loving men on horseback may have ridden into the sunset, but they have yet to ride out of our hearts.

And what did they eat, these knights of the trail? Well, there is no doubt, there were staples that lend themselves to a rather alliterative recounting—biscuits and beans, steak and stew, Arbuckle's and apple pie—all served by a cook with a disposition just the other side of outlaw-mean. But while he may have been ornery, any camp cook worth his salt took pride in what he set before the hands.

The biscuits were almost invariably the sourdough variety, most cowboys having little use for baking powder or buttermilk biscuits and even less for baker's bread. Most often they were prepared in the cook's most important and valuable utensil: the Dutch oven. As for beans, pinto beans, so-named for their brown spots, were most popular. Known as *frijoles* to the southwesterners and as Mexican strawberries to most cowboys, beans, also cooked in the ever-present Dutch oven, were so commonly part of the cowboy's chuck that dinnertime was often called "bean time" by the hands.

The steaks may have been beef but could just as easily have been venison or buffalo, some cattle owners being of the belief that unless an animal was either infirm or completely unmanageable (or belonged to somebody else), it had better still be part of the herd at the end of the drive. The saying "No Texan ever eats his own beef" probably had more than a little truth in its origin. One thing was sure: the steaks would be fried. It seemed cowboys never tired of them cooked in that manner.

The stew, on the other hand, was seldom cooked the same way twice. It had its own personality and its own name. It was most commonly known as son-of-a-bitch stew, and theories about how the name came about are as varied as the animal parts that made up the dish. Perhaps one of the first cowboys to sample the stew said, "Son-of-a-bitch, that's good!" Maybe the concoction was named in honor of one of the originating cook's enemies or possibly the name came from how those with tender stomachs felt after eating it. Of course, when delicate ears were within hearing range, the more politically correct designation—son-of-a-gun stew—was (and still is) invoked.

Along with dinner and after the coffee flowed freely. As for dessert, well, there was no better way for the cook to win the undying loyalty of the trail hands than to muster up the occasional pie. The cowboy's sweet tooth wasn't satisfied by dipping his biscuits in molasses, and the mere thought of pie for dessert made the day on the trail go a whole lot faster. And, yep, more often than not, the pie was baked in that same Dutch oven.

The cowboy's chuck was, for the most part, simple fare. And because of the limited space of the chuckwagon, variety wasn't a feature of dining on the range. Although here again, the innovative rancher Charles Goodnight had an idea. Credited with inventing or at least redesigning the chuckwagon, Goodnight sometimes had his cooks plant gardens along the trail. The idea was that following drives would harvest the mature vegetables and, in turn, plant another garden in their place.

Mealtime wasn't just about nourishment. It provided an important and welcome diversion from the trail's endless and often dangerous challenges, some natural, some manmade.

Meals provided an opportunity for fellowship, rest and at least a few moments of peace before the trail hands mounted up again, ready to face whatever lay ahead.

It is not an exaggeration to suggest that the wagon cook and what he produced were in large part responsible for the cowboy's contentment with life. It is in that spirit that we offer these recipes to you. They have come from the ranches, restaurants and people of the West. Many of the recipes reflect the same enterprising, inventive attitude that was so important in the development of the western way of life. And, like the movement of cattle, the recipes in this book follow a northward progression from the Rio Grande River at the southern tip of Texas to the Peace River in Canada.

So good eatin' to ya. Nobody's ever said it better than those camp cooks of a century ago: "Come and get it."

The Southwest

Arizona, New Mexico, Texas

WITH ITS CHARACTERISTIC BOLD FLAVORS AND BRIGHT colors, food in the Southwest tradition has become increasingly popular. More and more restaurants on both sides of the 49th parallel boast Southwest or Tex-Mex cookery. The food of the entire region is a delightful mix of Native American and ethnic influences. The Native Americans lived on a simple diet of foods such as corn, squash and beans. Spanish missionaries traveling north into the region introduced chilies, onions, garlic, tomatoes, wheat, rice and orchard fruits. All of these influences have given the region's cuisine a richness and variety that is sometimes forgotten in the haste of outsiders to stamp everything that's "hot, spicy and bean-based" as Southwestern fare. While the region's two main influences are Native American and ethnic, local specialties have developed. In Arizona you are more likely to find wheat tortillas than corn. New Mexicans prefer to stack their enchiladas, like a torte.

Texas salsas will often have cooked tomatoes as their base rather than raw tomatoes. And around San Antonio, where German settlers have put their stamp on the region's food, you might find tacos served with shredded cabbage rather than the traditional lettuce.

There are only a few things to know in order to successfully recreate the dishes of the Southwest. The first and maybe most important is the difference between chile with an *e* and chili with an *i*. The former is the name of the plant with its more than two hundred varieties. Though it is often called a pepper, it is not a form of the plant that produces black pepper; in fact, not even close. While it is known quite rightly for its heat, the chile is every bit as important for its flavor. Chili with an *i*, on the other hand, has a couple of designations. It is the packaged powder made up of chiles, cumin, oregano, garlic and other spices. It also denotes the dish made with chiles and meat, which most of us in the northern parts of the continent associate with Mexican food. Widely known as chili con carne, it is most often referred to as a "bowl of red" in Texas. The debate rages on about whether real chili should be made with beans or without, although the stuff of Chili-Cookoff World Championships is definitely beanless.

The importance of corn cannot be overemphasized in dishes of the Southwest. Given the influence of the Hopi, Navajo, Pueblo and Zuni Indians, it's not surprising that this versatile vegetable has had such an impact on the cuisine of the Southwest. Blue corn is especially popular in New Mexico, while the more common yellow variety is found elsewhere in the region.

Tortillas, the flat discs made either from flour or masa harina (a corn-based flour), are another staple. An Indian invention, tortillas have become as much a part of the everyday diet of the region's residents as pita is to Greeks and freshly baked bread is to Canadians. Wrapping tortillas around various combinations of beans, chicken, beef, tomatoes, potatoes, fruit, nuts and chiles creates burritos, chimichangas and enchiladas. In New Mexico tortillas are most likely made from corn; in Arizona they're made from wheat, a grain first introduced by the Spaniards.

Almost as important to the Southwestern diet as tortillas are *frijoles refritos* or refried beans, with the pinto bean being the preferred source. Add a little chorizo sausage and some cornbread and presto (make that *ole!*), you're in the Southwest.

Not to be overlooked is the popularity of the barbecue. The word comes from the Spanish *barbacoa*, but the practice of slow cooking over heated coals is Indian in origin. In a climate that permits both cooking and eating outdoors virtually year round, barbecues are a never-ending culinary pastime, and in Texas, mesquite wood has become synonymous with barbecuing. Most of us know a little about mesquite, having enjoyed its effects in one of the countless Tex-Mex restaurants that have sprung up all over North America. What is not as well known is that this hardy plant is one of the hottest burning hardwoods on the planet. More bush than tree, the mesquite imparts a distinctive, smoky flavor to whatever is cooked over its flames, and it is this that makes it special. To barbecue-loving Texans especially, the ugly mesquite plant is almost as cherished as the lovely blue bonnets that cover the hills and fields in spring and summer.

Not every item on the Southwest menu is spicy or exotic. Favorites like chicken-fried steak, black-eyed peas and fried catfish border on the ordinary—until the first mouthful. But the truth is, most Southwest dishes tend to be on the hot side. That might explain, at least in part, why a sweet ending to a meal is both a popular and long-standing tradition in the area.

All right, that's enough talk about Southwestern cuisine. Let's get down to some serious cooking. First a couple of hints. When working with chiles, rubber gloves are a must in order to avoid burns to the skin. And forget all that stuff about having a cold beer or two handy to diminish the fiery effects of the chiles. Milk or a dollop of sour cream is actually more effective.

[Starters]

Ranch Mustard

Marijo Balmer
Folsom Falls Ranch, Folsom, New Mexico

A tangy condiment for ham or pork, this recipe can also be used as a sandwich spread.

MAKES 1 CUP

½ cup	dry mustard
½ cup	wine vinegar
1	egg, beaten
½ cup	sugar
	mayonnaise to taste

๛ Mix mustard and vinegar together and let stand overnight. When ready to use, combine all ingredients in top of double boiler and cook until mixture coats a spoon. Cool and add enough mayonnaise to equal mustard mixture, or to taste.

Cowpatty Dip

Gala Nettles
Nettles Cutting Horses, Madisonville, Texas

While writing her book about the King Ranch and world champion cutting horse Little Peppy, Gala lived right at the ranch. She liked this appetizer recipe so much she brought it home with her.

SERVES 6 TO 8

1 cup	sour cream
1 tbsp	taco seasoning
2	10 oz cans bean dip
	guacamole (recipe page 26)
1	4 oz can black olives, chopped
1	small onion, chopped
1	tomato, chopped
2 cups	cheese, grated

☙ Combine sour cream and taco seasoning in a small bowl. Spread bean dip on a large platter. Layer guacamole, sour cream mixture, olives, onions, tomato and cheese over bean dip. Chill until serving time. Serve with tortilla chips.

Pico de Gallo

Fresh tomato salsa brimming with the flavors of peppers and cilantro is a necessary accompaniment to crisp-fried tortilla chips.

MAKES 2 CUPS

4	large tomatoes, chopped
½ cup	green onions, finely chopped
2	jalapeno peppers, finely chopped
2	cloves garlic, minced
¼ cup	lime juice
½ cup	cilantro, finely chopped
1 tsp	oregano
	salt and pepper to taste

❧ Combine all ingredients. Cover and refrigerate until serving time. This is best when made less than 3 hours before serving.

Guacamole Estupendo

Guacamole works as a dip on its own or as a flavorful addition to other Southwest dishes.

SERVES 6 TO 8

2	ripe avocados
1 tbsp	lime juice
2	cloves garlic, crushed
1 tbsp	pickled jalapeno pepper, finely chopped
1 cup	sour cream
⅛ tsp	cumin
¼ tsp	salt
1	large tomato, chopped, drained
3	green onions, chopped
1	large green bell pepper, chopped

❧ Peel and mash avocados. Add lime juice immediately to prevent avocado from darkening, then add garlic, jalapeno, sour cream, cumin and salt. Mix well with an electric mixer. Add tomatoes, onion and green pepper and mix by hand. Chill for 2 hours before serving.

Mexican Hash Dip

Marijo Balmer
Folsom Falls Ranch, Folsom, New Mexico

Serve this tasty dip with tortilla chips and mugs of beer.

SERVES 4 TO 6

2	4 oz cans crushed olives
1	4 oz can green chiles, diced
1	4 oz can mushrooms, diced
½ cup	onions, diced
½ cup	tomatoes, diced
— or —	
½ cup	salsa
1 tbsp	olive oil
2 tbsp	wine vinegar

🍂 Combine ingredients and mix well. Enjoy!

Chorizo Cheese Dip

This dip is a fabulous starter when served warm from the oven with fresh tortilla chips and red wine!

SERVES 8 TO 12

1 lb	chorizo sausage meat
1	medium onion, finely chopped
1	clove garlic, minced
½ cup	celery, finely chopped
½	red or green bell pepper, finely chopped
1 cup	mushrooms, finely chopped
¾ to 1 cup	tomato juice
2 to 3 tbsp	jalapeno pepper, chopped
1 ½ cups	Jack cheese, grated
1 ½ cups	Cheddar cheese, grated
	tortilla chips

❧ Cook chorizo, onion and garlic. Drain excess fat, then add celery, peppers, mushrooms and tomato juice. Simmer until vegetables are tender and liquid cooks down. Add jalapeno pepper and grated cheeses and stir until melted. Serve warm with tortilla chips. This recipe can be made ahead and refrigerated. Heat before serving.

Sweet and Sour Sausages

Gala Nettles
Nettles Cutting Horses, Madisonville, Texas

Gala ran across this recipe while on a horse-searching expedition. One minute the lady of the house was at the barn showing her horses; five minutes later she was serving this snack with drinks. The trick is to keep sliced sausage in the freezer for such occasions.

SERVES 6

1	package smoked sausage
1 tbsp	mustard, to taste
1	8 oz jar apple jelly

&. Slice sausage into bite-size pieces and set aside. Combine mustard and jelly in a saucepan and heat until both are dissolved, making a sweet and sour sauce. Add sausages and heat until warm. Serve with crackers as an appetizer or with rice as a main course.

Quesadillas

Filled with cheese and peppers, quesadillas are a traditional Southwest appetizer.

SERVES 8

½ cup	Jack or Cheddar cheese, grated
1	jalapeno pepper, roasted, chopped
1	small tomato, sliced (optional)
1	grilled chicken breast, diced (optional)
2	large flour tortillas

🍃 Layer cheese and jalapeno on top of one tortilla. Add tomato and grilled chicken, if desired. Cover with the other tortilla. Heat a bit of oil in a frying pan and fry for 2 minutes on one side. As it cooks, it may be necessary to weigh down the quesadilla with a small frying pan or heat-proof plate. Turn the quesadilla over and fry for another 2 minutes. Drain on paper towels. Cut into triangles and serve with guacamole, sour cream or salsa.

The Range Cook

It is no exaggeration to say that the chuckwagon cook was as important to the success of the trail drive as any man on it. He may have been cantankerous, cranky and even a tad crazy, but if he was a capable cook all else was forgiven, and peace and harmony were likely to reign over the drive.

Considering the job description of the cowboy cook, it should come as no surprise that his disposition tended to be on the feisty side. As one old-timer put it, "If a camp cook ain't grouchy, he ain't been cookin' long enough." Feeding up to twenty hungry cowboys, preparing food in weather conditions that would drive a duck indoors, slinging cast iron cooking utensils, and keeping the food supplies relatively free of dust, mud, flies and axle grease would try anyone's patience.

The range cook's duties went far beyond those of a ranch cook. On the trail, the cook had to be a teamster, doctor, sometimes dentist, counselor, blacksmith and veterinarian. In fact, the cook's last duty of the day was one of the most important. Each night he aimed the tongue of the chuckwagon in the direction of the north star, providing a kind of compass reference point for at least the beginning of the next day's drive.

The truth is that the legend of the grouchy cook is probably as much fable as fact. Some were as amiable as all get out, but the ones who were grumpy weren't to be messed with. Weak coffee, hard biscuits and a menu long on beans and short on sweets was likely to be the result of a disgruntled cook. But one fact is certain. The range cook was an unflinchingly loyal, tireless worker, whose contributions to the atmosphere and success of the trail drive were second to none. And if he wasn't cheerful, who really cared as long as the man kept the coffee hot and could make a decent biscuit.

[Breads]

Sourdough Biscuits

These biscuits can be baked ahead at the ranch and taken to the campsite, or they can be made up and baked in a Dutch oven over hot coals. If you opt for the latter, prepare the coals in plenty of time so they're ready for the Dutch oven.

SERVES 4 TO 6

1 cup	flour
½ tsp	baking soda
2 tsp	baking powder
½ tsp	salt
1 cup	sourdough starter (recipe next page)
⅓ cup	oil

❧ Stir together flour, baking soda, baking powder and salt. Add the sourdough starter and oil. Stir lightly, just until moistened.

❧ Turn out onto a lightly floured surface and pat out to ¾-inch thickness. Cut into 2-inch rounds. Bake on a greased baking sheet at 400° F for 12 to 15 minutes, or in a Dutch oven over hot coals until golden brown.

Sourdough Starter

This starter is easy for those just venturing into the world of sourdough cooking.

2 cups	flour
1 tbsp	dry yeast
1 tsp	salt
3 tbsp	white sugar
2 cups	lukewarm water

&~ Mix dry ingredients in a mixing bowl. Slowly add warm water, stirring until mixture is smooth. Cover bowl with a tea towel and set in a reasonably warm place for 3 full days. Stir mixture two or three times each day. The starter will be ready to use by the end of the third day. At this point, place the starter in a plastic container with a hole punched through the lid to allow gas to escape (1 quart ice cream container works well). Store in refrigerator.

&~ To use starter, stir well and remove desired amount. Replenish with ½ cup flour and ½ cup warm water after each use. Let stand at room temperature for about 24 hours, or overnight, before returning to refrigerator. This starter will last for years if used regularly. Make sure to occasionally pour starter into a bowl and wash plastic container to avoid crust that forms around edge.

Flour Tortillas

Tortillas are truly versatile. They can be used to wrap around beans, eggs or meat or layered in casseroles.

MAKES 36 TORTILLAS

6 cups	flour
1 tsp	baking powder
2 tsp	salt
1 heaping cup	vegetable shortening
2 cups	warm water

❧ Combine dry ingredients and shortening, then add water and mix until stiff. Let stand 30 minutes.

❧ Divide dough to make 36 tortillas. Knead individual tortillas using flour to avoid sticking. Roll with rolling pin, flipping sides after each roll across the tortilla. The tortillas should be about 1 inch in diameter and ⅛ to ¼-inches thick.

❧ Heat a griddle or a frying pan until hot. Cook tortillas until they are cooked through and have developed brown spots. Do not scorch. Lower heat as necessary to maintain an even temperature. The tortillas will puff up slightly as they cook. Turn and cook other side. When cooked, press edges down with a spatula for about 30 seconds to produce flat, golden disks that are crisp and tasty.

Hush Puppies

Hush puppies are a great Southern dish and a wonderful accompaniment to just about any entrée. The name originated when hunters, in an attempt to quiet their hungry hounds, threw bits of food at the dogs, yelling, "Hush, puppies."

SERVES 8

1 ½ cups	yellow cornmeal
½ cup	flour
2 tsp	baking powder
½ tsp	salt
⅛ tsp	pepper
1	egg, beaten
¾ cup	milk
1 tbsp	onion, minced

❧ Sift dry ingredients together. In a separate bowl, beat eggs and stir in milk and onion. Add egg mixture to dry ingredients and mix well.

❧ Heat oil in a frying pan. Drop batter into oil by heaping teaspoonfuls. Fry until golden, turning as they brown. Remove from pan and drain on paper towels. Serve hot.

Beer Muffins

These hearty muffins are excellent served with bowls of hot, spicy chili.

MAKES 12 MUFFINS

4 cups	biscuit mix
2 tbsp	sugar
1	12 oz can of beer

&. Combine ingredients and beat vigorously for 1 minute. Fill hot, greased muffin tins and bake at 400° F for about 15 minutes. Serve warm.

Navajo Fry Bread

This fried bread is delicious with jam or a dusting of powered sugar. If topped with ground beef, lettuce and salsa, it's called an Indian taco.

SERVES 5

4 cups	flour
1	package dry yeast
½ cup	milk
½ cup	sugar
¼ cup	water
1 tsp	salt
¼ cup	butter
2	eggs
	jam or powered sugar (optional)

&. Mix 1 ½ cups of flour with yeast and set aside. Heat milk, sugar, water, salt and butter until warm. Add to flour mixture along with eggs. Beat with mixer for about 3 minutes. Stir in as much flour as possible. The mixture should be neither too moist nor too dry.

&. Turn out onto a floured surface and knead in remaining flour. Shape into a ball and place in a greased bowl. Cover and refrigerate overnight.

&. Remove dough from refrigerator and let stand for 30 minutes. Punch down and turn onto a floured surface. Cover and let rest for 10 minutes. Roll dough into ¼-inch thickness and cut into 3 x 4-inch rectangles.

❧ Heat oil in a large frying pan and fry 2 rectangles at a time for about 2 minutes each, or until golden, turning once. Drain on paper towels.

❧ Spread with jam or sprinkle with powdered sugar and serve immediately. For variation, layer with taco mix.

Elfego Baca

While many of the West's most mythical shoot-outs were just that—myth—there was at least one that needed no Hollywood rewrite to put it into the category of larger-than-life.

Even in a land noted for spawning and attracting unusual men and women, Elfego Baca was unique. As a nineteen-year-old, the New Mexico wannabee lawman purchased a mail-order badge and promptly arrested a cowboy who was harassing Hispanic towns-folk. The arrest didn't sit well with the cowboy's ranch foreman, and he and eighty sympathizers rode out after Baca.

After gunning down one of his pursuers, the quasi-lawman took refuge in a mud and wood hut. The cowboys poured lead into the hut for the rest of that day. Luckily for Baca, he had selected the perfect hideout. The hut was equipped with a floor that lay twelve inches below ground level. It was there that Baca quite literally lay low, emerging from time to time to shoot back with enough accuracy to kill three more of the cowboys and wound several others.

Around midnight the frustrated cowboys destroyed most of the building with a well-placed stick of dynamite, then settled back to wait for daylight to check out the results of their work. Dawn came, but before the gunmen could move in they were astonished to see smoke rising from the chimney of what was left of the hut. The ever-practical Elfego Baca was cooking breakfast.

The shooting resumed and continued until late the next day when help finally arrived in the person of a real lawman. A later examination revealed 367 bullet holes in the hut's door alone.

Elfego Baca survived to become a prominent New Mexico lawyer.

Blue Corn Pancakes

If you want to impress your breakfast guests, whip up a spread of blue cornmeal pancakes and serve them with strawberry butter (recipe next page) and a side of chorizo sausage. Guaranteed they'll be back to visit again!

MAKES 12 PANCAKES

4	eggs
2 cups	buttermilk
2 tbsp	melted butter
1 ½ cups	blue cornmeal (available in health food or specialty stores)
1 cup	flour
1 tbsp	baking powder
1 tbsp	sugar
½ tsp	salt
1 ½ cups	fresh or frozen corn kernels

❧ Combine eggs, buttermilk and melted butter and blend well. Slowly stir in dry ingredients. Add corn. Preheat a griddle or a frying pan. Spoon batter into pan and cook pancakes, about 2 minutes per side. Serve immediately.

Whipped Strawberry Butter

½ to 1 cup   butter, softened
1 to 2 generous tbsp   strawberry jam

❦ Using an electric mixer, blend jam and butter. Serve with pancakes.

Crispy Waffles

Pecans are found in abundance in the South and add a delicious crunch to these breakfast waffles.

SERVES 4

2 cups   biscuit mix
1   egg
½ cup   oil
1 ⅓ cup   club soda
⅓ cup   pecans, finely chopped

❦ Combine all ingredients except pecans and mix well. Pour batter, ¼ cup at a time, onto a hot waffle iron. Serve waffles with whipped cream, fresh fruit, fruit topping or syrup. Sprinkle pecans on top.

Pecan Caramel Coffee Rolls

Pecans are one of the largest crops in the American South and add a great taste to these lovely rolls. A sweet treat for breakfast with a steaming cup of coffee or anytime the mood strikes.

SERVES 6

1	package frozen dinner rolls
1	package instant butterscotch pudding
½ cup	brown sugar
½ cup	butter
½ cup	pecans, chopped

❧ Place frozen rolls in a Bundt or angel food pan. Sprinkle pudding on top of rolls. Bring brown sugar and butter to a boil and pour over rolls. Sprinkle nuts on top. Put in oven overnight. The next morning, set the oven to 350° F (with rolls still in oven) and bake for 25 minutes.

Southern Apricot Loaf

This loaf is great as a quick breakfast if you're in a hurry or as a late afternoon snack with tea.

SERVES 12

¾ cup	flour
1 cup	sugar
½ tsp	baking powder
½ tsp	salt
¾ cup	Grapenuts cereal
⅔ cup	dried apricots, chopped
1	egg, beaten
1 ¼ cups	milk
2 tbsp	vegetable oil

❧ In a large bowl, mix together the first 6 ingredients. In a small bowl, blend egg, milk and oil. Stir into the first mixture just until moistened. Spoon mixture into a greased loaf pan.

❧ Bake at 350° F for 1 hour, or until done. Cool in pan and store overnight for easier slicing. Serve with whipped cream cheese for a real Southern taste.

[Salads & Side Dishes]

Lone Star Caviar

Dennis and Charlene Semkin
Semkin Longhorns, Prescott, Arizona

Found in an old family cookbook, this recipe can be served as either a side dish or a summer salad. Black-eyed peas are grown in abundance throughout Texas and celebrated each year at the Black-Eyed Pea Jamboree in Athens, Texas.

SERVES 6 TO 8

1 lb	dry black-eyed peas
2 cups	Italian salad dressing (non-creamy)
2 cups	green peppers, chopped
1 ½ cups	onions, diced
	salt to taste
	hot pepper sauce to taste
1 cup	green onions, chopped
½ cup	jalapeno pepper, finely chopped
3 oz	pimento, drained, diced
1 tbsp	fresh garlic, minced

⊱ Soak peas for 6 hours or overnight. Drain. Transfer to a saucepan and add water to cover. Bring to a boil over high heat. Reduce heat and allow to boil until tender, about 45 minutes. Do not overcook. Drain well and transfer to a large bowl. Add dressing and cool. Add remaining ingredients and mix well.

Hot Bean Salad

Beans were a staple of the early settlers in Texas. This combination adds color and flavor galore!

SERVES 4

4	slices bacon, cooked crisp, crumbled
½ cup	sugar
1 tbsp	cornstarch
1 tsp	salt
¼ tsp	pepper
⅔ cup	vinegar
1	16 oz can green beans, drained
1	16 oz can yellow beans, drained
1	16 oz can red kidney beans, drained
1	onion, sliced

❧ Cook bacon well, drain and crumble. Set aside. Combine sugar and cornstarch in a saucepan and stir. Add salt, pepper and vinegar. Cook over medium heat, stirring until thickened. Add beans and onion and cook for a few more minutes. Sprinkle crumbled bacon on top before serving.

Tex-Mex Salad

The combination of corn and peppers gives this salad its Tex-Mex flavor. As pretty to look at as it is delicious to eat, it goes well with any roasted meat.

SERVES 4 TO 6

2	14 oz cans kernel corn, drained
1	small onion, minced
2 to 3	raw carrots, finely chopped
½	green pepper, finely chopped
½	red pepper, finely chopped
4	hard-boiled eggs, chopped
	salt and pepper to taste
½ to 1 cup	mayonnaise

&. Combine all ingredients and refrigerate until ready to serve.

Black-Eyed Pea Salad

The addition of picante sauce heats up this dish. This salad goes well with barbecued ribs.

SERVES 8

3	16 oz cans black-eyed peas, drained
1	large tomato, diced
1	large green or red bell pepper, diced
1	large red onion, diced
2 tbsp	picante sauce (or salsa)
4 heaping tbsp	mayonnaise

ᶻ Combine all ingredients and refrigerate until serving time.

Mexican Spinach Salad

Coriander leaves give this spinach salad a unique flavor.

SERVES 6 TO 8

3	bunches fresh spinach
½ cup	green onions, chopped
⅓ cup	fresh coriander leaves
— or —	
1 tsp	ground coriander
½ cup	Mexican-style salad dressing (recipe next page)
	cherry tomatoes or sliced radishes for garnish

❧ Wash spinach, drain and dry leaves well. Roll in paper towels until ready to use. To prepare salad, discard spinach stems and tear leaves into a large salad bowl.

❧ Chop green onions and coriander leaves. Toss with spinach and add salad dressing. Garnish with cherry tomatoes or radishes. Serve immediately.

Mexican-Style Salad Dressing

This dressing complements any vegetable salad nicely.

½ cup	olive oil
½ cup	vegetable oil
⅓ cup	wine vinegar
½ tsp	salt
1 tsp	garlic, crushed
1 tsp	rosemary
¼ cup	ice water

🥢 Combine all ingredients in a jar and shake well. Chill in refrigerator at least 4 hours or overnight to ripen flavors, especially the rosemary. Strain over salad.

Chayote Salad

Chayote is a pear-shaped, light green vegetable commonly used in Southwest cooking and has a somewhat delicate flavor that is nicley complemented by ingredients with a bit of bite.

SERVES 6 TO 8

3	chayotes
6 cups	water
1 tsp	salt
1 cup	purple onion, sliced
¼ cup	vinegar
¾ cup	oil
1	clove garlic, crushed
	salt and pepper to taste
1 tsp	oregano leaves, crushed
	pickled red jalapeno strips and black olives for garnish

❧ Cut chayotes in half lengthwise and boil in salted water until tender, about 1 hour. Drain and cool. Peel and slice in long, thin slices.

❧ Blanch onion slices with 2 cups boiling water. Drain. Marinate onions for 2 hours in mixture of vinegar, oil, garlic, salt and pepper. Sprinkle with crushed oregano.

❧ Arrange chayote slices on a large platter and add onion slices to cover. Drizzle marinade over salad. Garnish with strips of red jalapeno chiles and a few black olives.

Potato Salad

This is a slightly different version of potato salad. Sprinkle with oregano leaves and garnish with chile strips. The salad will keep in the refrigerator for several days.

SERVES 8

4	potatoes
¼ cup	vinegar
½ cup	oil
1 tsp	prepared mustard
	salt and pepper to taste
1 tsp	dry oregano
— or —	
1 tbsp	fresh oregano leaves
1 tbsp	chili strips
¼ cup	green onion, chopped

❧ Boil the unpeeled potatoes until tender but not mushy. Peel and slice when cool. Place in salad bowl. Combine vinegar, oil, mustard, and salt and pepper in a jar and shake, making sure mustard is well mixed. Pour over sliced potatoes and mix together carefully. Sprinkle oregano, chili strips and green onion over top for garnish. Keep chilled until ready to serve.

Fluffy Potato Casserole

Bob Tallman
Bandana Braford Ranch, Weatherford, Texas

Bob Tallman, National Finals Rodeo announcer and several times Professional Rodeo Cowboy Association Announcer of the Year, claims this recipe as one of his favorites. His wife, Kristen, says it's easy to make and a great choice for cowboy or family gatherings. It's also an easy dish to prepare for unexpected company "because it's quick fixin's."

SERVES 6 TO 8

4 cups	cooked potatoes, mashed
2 tbsp	butter
2	8 oz packages cream cheese, softened
4	eggs
4 tbsp	flour
	salt and pepper to taste
1	large onion, finely chopped
2	cans French-fried onion rings

❧ Mash cooked potatoes with butter (don't add milk). Add softened cream cheese and beat until smooth. Add eggs, flour, salt and pepper and beat until fluffy. Fold in chopped onion and mix well. Place in a large casserole dish. Casserole can be made to this point until ready to bake. Bake at 325° F for 1 hour, or until fluffy, set and light golden in color. Top with French-fried onion rings and bake another 5 minutes.

Dirty Rice

Fred Balmer
Folsom Falls Ranch, Folsom, New Mexico

This Southern dish gets its name from the color of the rice once it's cooked. It can stand alone as a main meal with a green salad or fits well as a side dish to accompany any barbecued meat.

SERVES 4 TO 6

1 cup	uncooked old-fashioned rice
— or —	
2 cups	minute rice
3	slices bacon, diced, cooked
1	16 oz can black beans
½	4 oz can green chiles, diced
1	beef bouillon cube
1 tsp	onion, diced
1 tbsp	butter
¼ tsp	chili powder

&. Cook rice. Dice, cook and drain bacon. Combine all ingredients and mix well. Serve immediately.

Santa Fe Rice

This recipe is a tried and true Southwest favorite.

Serves 12

4 cups	brown rice, cooked
2 cups	celery, sliced
1 cup	kernel corn
1 cup	green or white onions, sliced
1 ½ cups	green or red pepper, sliced
1 cup	sunflower seeds
1 cup	almonds
1 cup	raisins
¼ cup	soy sauce
¼ cup	chicken broth
¾ lb	white Cheddar cheese, grated

&❧ Cook rice. Combine vegetables, sunflower seeds, almonds and raisins in a large casserole or baking dish. Pour soy sauce and chicken broth over top. Sprinkle with cheese. Spread brown rice evenly over top. Bake at 250° F for 20 minutes, or until well heated. Toss gently before serving.

Frijoles Refritos

Refried beans are great as a side dish along with rice and burritos or enchiladas.

SERVES 4

2 cups	cooked pinto beans
	water
1	clove garlic, crushed
1 tbsp	onion, chopped
	salt to taste
2 tsp	oil
1 cup	Longhorn cheese, grated (may substitute Jack cheese)

❧ Mash beans with a potato masher. Add a little water, garlic, onion and salt. Cook bean mixture in hot oil until thoroughly heated. Add more water as necessary to keep mixture from drying out. Add cheese and cook until melted. Serve hot.

[Main Dishes]

Hozro Ranch Stew

Bill Lyons
Lyons Ranch, Zavala County, Texas

The Lyons family serves up this tasty stew at their ranch during hunting season.

SERVES 8 TO 10

2 lbs	ground beef or venison
2	onions, chopped
2	14 oz cans ranch-style pork and beans
2	14 oz cans whole kernel corn, drained
2	14 oz cans tomatoes, diced
	green chiles to taste
	salt and pepper to taste

🌢 Cook ground meat and onions in a large frying pan. Add remaining ingredients. Simmer to remove excess moisture and seep flavors into the meat. The Lyons family says the stew tastes even better the next day.

Son-of-a-Bitch Stew

This dish evolved from cowboy cooks watching Native Americans, whose practice was to cook and eat the organs of the animals they hunted and leave the muscles for predatory animals.

SERVES 8 TO 10

1 lb	beef
1 ½ lbs	beef liver
½	beef heart
1 set	marrow gut
1 set	sweetbreads
1 set	brains
2	large onions, minced
1	clove garlic, minced
1 tbsp	chili powder
	salt and pepper to taste

❧ Cut beef, liver and heart into 1-inch cubes. Slice marrow gut into small rings. Place all pieces in a Dutch oven, cover meat with water and simmer 2 to 3 hours. Add onions, garlic, chili powder, and salt and pepper to taste.

❧ Cut sweetbreads and brains into small pieces and add to stew. Simmer, don't boil, for another hour. Serve with biscuits.

Kit Carson

As is the case with many of the legendary characters of the Old West, opinion is divided on whether Kit Carson was hero, villain or parts of each. Earp, Holliday, Masterson, Custer and even Jesse James and Billy the Kid all fall into that category of men whose characters were made up of equal parts good and evil.

Christopher Houston (Kit) Carson was an early trapper, frontier scout and trail blazer. In those capacities there is no doubt that he, along with the likes of famed mountain man Jim Bridger, played as vital a role in opening up the West as the wagon trains that overcame endless hardships to bring settlers to the vast, untamed land. In fact, Carson scouted for John Charles Fremont, who mapped the all-important Oregon Trail.

It was in his later years as an Indian fighter that Carson's career became more controversial. In 1864 (now Colonel) Kit Carson, after forcing the Navajo into submission by destroying their crops and livestock, led them on a forced three-hundred-mile march from the country around Canyon de Chelly to Bosque Redondo in the southern part of New Mexico. The march, which became known to the Navajo as the Long Walk, resulted in massive casualties to the Indians. So did the almost uninhabitable land around Bosque Redondo. But by 1868 the resilient Navajo had returned to their homelands and have since become one of the populous nations in North America.

But while the debate rages on about the decency and effectiveness of Kit Carson's career as an Indian fighter, there is one aspect of the Carson legend that has no controversy connected with it. Like so many of the West's early residents Kit Carson loved his chili, so much so that, as the story goes, his dying words were, "I wish there was time for just one more bowl of chili."

Green Chili With Beef

A traditional beanless chili, this versatile dish can be used as a filling for burritos or served as a main course with baked potatoes, a fresh garden salad and warm tortillas.

SERVES 2 TO 3

1 lb	beef round
4 cups	water
1 tsp	salt
	pinch of pepper
2	cloves garlic, crushed
½ cup	onion, chopped
2 tbsp	oil
½ cup	ripe tomato, peeled, chopped
4	green chile peppers, roasted, chopped
— or —	
1	4 oz can green chiles, chopped

&. Cut beef in large pieces. In a large saucepan, add beef, water, salt, pepper and garlic and cook for 1 hour, or until tender and well done. Allow to cool in broth. Drain, reserving broth. Chop beef into small pieces and set aside.

&. In a large frying pan, sauté onion in oil. Do not allow to brown. Add tomato, green chiles and 1 cup of reserved broth. Bring to a simmer and cook for 3 minutes. Add the beef and adjust seasonings. Allow to cook for about 5 minutes more, or until liquid boils down.

Chili Con Carne

Casa Rio Restaurant
San Antonio, Texas

One of the oldest restaurants on San Antonio's renowned River Walk, Casa Rio features traditional Mexican food. Locals and tourists alike stop in for their most famous dish—chili con carne.

Chili originated in San Antonio as a way to serve the tougher Texas longhorn steer meat. The cubed meat distinguishes Texas chili from other versions.

SERVES 40 TO 50

20 lbs	beef or venison, cubed
10 lbs	pork, cubed
4 oz	hot serrano pepper, ground
4 oz	fresh garlic, minced
½ cup	salt
2 cups	fresh chili pods, ground
⅓ cups	black pepper, freshly ground
1 to 1 ½ cups	chili powder

&. Place beef and pork in a 6 gallon cooking pot. Fill the pot with water until the meat is just covered. Add remaining ingredients except chili powder.

&. Bring to a boil and cook meat until very tender. Add chili powder and mix well. Remove from heat and set aside to cool. Just before serving, return to heat and thicken with a roux of two parts flour to one part lard.

A Bowl of Red

Chili is the official dish of Texas and known as "a bowl of red."

SERVES 4 TO 6

1 ½ to 2 lbs	flank or sirloin steak
	flour
	oil
1 cup	beer
⅓ cup	cooking sherry or red wine
1	14 oz can tomatoes
1	large onion, chopped
2	cloves garlic, finely minced
4 stalks	celery, chopped
1	red pepper, chopped
2 to 3	jalapeno peppers, chopped
2 tbsp	honey
1 to 2 tsp	cumin
2 to 3 tsp	chili powder
2	bay leaves
1 to 2 tbsp	lime juice
	black pepper, freshly ground

ᴥ Cut meat into strips, roll in flour and fry in hot oil. Remove from pan and place in a large bowl. Add beer and sherry and let sit overnight in refrigerator.

ᴥ Next day, transfer to a heavy pot and add remaining ingredients. Simmer long and slow to blend flavors. If chili is too soupy, thicken with cornstarch mixed with some chili juices.

Cajun Beans

Cajun flavors from Louisiana permeate this hearty bean dish.

SERVES 6 TO 9

3 cups	pinto beans
1	ham hock
1	smoked sausage, cut into bite-sized pieces
1	large onion, diced
3	stalks celery, diced
1	bell pepper, diced
	salt and pepper to taste
1 cup	raw rice
2 cups	cheese, grated

🥬 Cook beans and ham hock until nearly done, about 4 hours. Add remaining ingredients except rice and cheese. Continue cooking until done, 30 to 60 minutes. Remove ham hock.

🥬 Cook rice according to package directions and put into a casserole dish. Spoon beans over rice, being sure to add lots of the bean juice. The rice will soak up the juice. Top the mixture with cheese. Put in a 350° F oven until cheese melts.

Barbecued Beef Brisket

Southwestern barbecues or barbacoa (which means slow roasting over pits of mesquite or coals) evolved from the Spaniards and Native Americans. The process often involved a double-sauce method. For tender, flavorful meat, baste the meat with one sauce while barbecuing and use the second as a serving accompaniment.

1	beef brisket or roast (3 to 4 lbs)
1 tbsp	seasoning salt
1 tsp ea	pepper, garlic powder, paprika

☙ Combine spices and rub into roast. While spiced roast sits, light mesquite chips or barbecue coals. Once chips or coals have burned down to form a slow fire, place roast on rack. Put about an inch of water in a dripping pan and place on the rack just below the roast. Cook roast slowly for about 2 ½ to 3 hours, basting every 20 minutes with the basting sauce (recipe below).

Basting Sauce

2 tbsp	olive oil
⅓ cup	red wine
1 tbsp	Worcestershire sauce
1	clove garlic, minced
1 tbsp	vinegar
1 tsp	dry mustard
½ tsp	cumin
½ tsp	coriander seed
¼ tsp	red pepper flakes
1 tsp	pepper

❧ Combine all ingredients well and use to baste meat as it cooks. Once beef is cooked, slice and serve with the following sauce.

Red Barbecue Sauce

½ cup	onion, finely chopped
¼ cup	celery, finely chopped
1 cup	ketchup
2 tbsp	honey
1 tbsp	Worcestershire sauce
1	clove garlic, minced
⅛ tsp	ground nutmeg
¼ tsp ea	ground cinnamon, cloves, ginger
1 tsp	pepper

❧ Combine all ingredients in a saucepan. Bring to a boil, then simmer for 10 to 15 minutes. Serve warm with sliced brisket.

Roast Goose à l'Orange

Pat Hutcherson
San Antonio, Texas

This unique Roast Goose à l'Orange came to us from a friend of Bill Lyons (of Lyons Ranch and Casa Rio restaurant).

SERVES 10 TO 12

2	large geese (8 to 10 lbs each)
1 cup	celery, chopped
½ cup	green onions, chopped
2 cups	apple, sliced
1 cup	apricots, chopped
2	garlic cloves, minced
	salt and pepper to taste
8 to 10	slices bacon
1 cup	orange juice concentrate
½ cup	red wine (optional)

❧ Wash and dry geese (duck or pheasant may be substituted). Stuff each cavity with mixture of celery, onion, apple, apricots and garlic. Salt and pepper geese and place bacon strips across the breasts. Dilute orange juice with one can of water and pour over geese.

❧ Cover with foil and marinate overnight. Bake at 450° F for 15 minutes, or until geese are slightly brown and bacon is crisp. Reduce heat to 250° F and cook for about 2 hours, or until geese are tender. Serve with wild rice.

Dutch Oven Pot Roast

Bob Martin
Dry Creek Ranch, Spur, Texas

Bob's Grandfather, Forrest Martin, cooked this dish at family get-togethers and cattle workings. Dutch oven cooking is an art requiring a bed of carefully prepared coals and a heavy fireproof Dutch oven.

SERVES 10 TO 12

1	5 lb rump roast
	flour
	salt and pepper to taste
½ cup	oil
2 to 3 cups	water

❧ Cut meat into fist-size chunks. Combine flour, salt and pepper and dredge meat in mixture. Heat oil in hot Dutch oven and brown meat chunks. Add water, then cover pot and cook slowly. Add additional water to keep gravy mixture around roast bubbling.

❧ Keep hot coals around Dutch oven. Stir and turn meat often to prevent sticking. Cook about 3 hours. Serve with baked potatoes, salad and biscuits.

Texas Hill-Country Quail, Family-Style

Please keep in mind that this recipe takes quite a few months to prepare, so start well in advance.

Prepare in the following order:

1. At least eight pointer bird dogs.
2. At least two 12-gauge shotguns.
3. At least two 20-gauge shotguns.
4. Several cases of shotgun shells for both 12- and 20-gauge guns.
5. Starting at 10:00 PM to about 1:30 AM, the children are to clean and dress several dozen freshly killed quail. This happens nightly. The late hour makes the flavor better.
6. The wife then checks for BB shot and extra feathers.
7. Put aside enough quail for meal and freeze the rest in water for later use. Soak quail in salt water for several hours.
8. Dip the quail in buttermilk and roll in flour. Add 1 tablespoon jalapeno juice to grease while frying quail. This adds a zesty flavor. Fry on both sides until brown and tender.
9. Serve with fried potatoes, buttermilk biscuits and milk gravy.

Calf Fries

*Just as salt water oysters are a delicacy for seafood lovers, calf fries
(also known further north as prairie or Rocky Mountain oysters)
are one of the traditional rewards at the close of a hard day's branding and castrating. While some city folks may turn up their noses at
the thought of dining on calves' testicles, once they have sampled a
well-prepared version of this dish, they're likely to be at the front of
the line next time around.*

&. Allow 3 to 4 calf fries per person as an appetizer, more for
a meal. Raw calf fries should be fresh, firm and have no yellow
color.

&. Cut into small pieces, roll or shake in a paper bag with
cornmeal, salt, pepper and a little garlic powder.

&. Fry in deep oil, drain and let rest in a warm oven until ready
to serve. If serving as an appetizer have some shrimp cocktail
sauce ready for dipping. Serve with mashed potatoes and salad
for a meal.

Chicken-Fried Steak

Steve Amos
Trinidad, Texas

What makes steak chicken-fried is dredging it in flour and cooking it in hot oil—just like fried chicken.

SERVES 4 TO 6

1 ½ lb	beef round steak
½ cup	flour
½ tsp	salt
¼ tsp	pepper
½ cup	vegetable oil
1 cup	milk
1 cup	water
	country gravy (recipe below)

🍂 Pound steak with meat mallet to ⅛-inch thickness. Combine flour, salt and pepper and dredge meat in mixture. Heat oil over medium heat in a large skillet. Cook meat 10 minutes on each side, or until browned. Remove from pan. Drain excess fat and keep steaks warm. Serve with mashed potatoes, biscuits and country gravy.

Country Gravy

🍂 For country gravy, melt 2 to 3 tablespoons shortening (or steak drippings) in pan. Stir in enough flour to form a paste. Slowly add milk or cream until mixture thickens. Salt and pepper to taste.

Beef and Artichoke Sauté

This is an easy dish to prepare when you're in a hurry.

SERVES 2

1	large onion
1	large red pepper
1 ½ lbs	beef rib eye or top round steak
1	6 oz jar marinated artichoke hearts
2 tbsp	ketchup
1 tsp	cornstarch
¼ tsp	instant chicken bouillon
¼ cup	water

◆ Cut onion into 8 wedges and separate layers. Cut red pepper into 1-inch wide strips. Slice steak on an angle into ⅛-inch thick strips.

◆ Drain artichokes, reserving marinade. Set 2 tablespoons marinade aside. Pour remaining marinade into a small bowl. Stir in ketchup, cornstarch, bouillon, and water. Add beef strips.

◆ In a frying pan over medium-high heat, heat the 2 tablespoons marinade until hot. Add onion and red pepper and cook until tender-crisp, stirring frequently. Use a slotted spoon to remove vegetables to plate. Add beef to frying pan and cook over high heat, stirring constantly, until meat loses its pink color. Add vegetables and artichoke hearts and cook over high heat just until heated through.

Cedar Creek Catfish Fry

Nan McHalek Creel
Dallas, Texas

Nan edited a cookbook herself not long ago: The Wolf Trapper's
Cookbook. *It's a good one. Catfish is a Southern favorite. If
unavailable, any white-fleshed fish may be substituted.*

SERVES 4

4 lbs	catfish filets
3	eggs, lightly beaten
1 tsp	salt
1 tsp	pepper
2 tsp	chili powder
1 cup	yellow cornmeal

⁂ Clean, skin and filet catfish. Mix eggs, salt, pepper and chili
powder together. Dip fish fillets in egg mixture until covered.
Dredge thoroughly in cornmeal. Pan fry in deep oil until flaky,
about 7 or 8 minutes.

Texas Fajitas

Fajitas are a Texas specialty.

SERVES 4

1 lb	round steak
¾ cup	oil
2 tbsp	red wine vinegar
2 tbsp	green onions, minced
¼ cup	honey
¼ cup	soy sauce
1 tsp	ground ginger
½ tsp	garlic powder
1 dozen	corn tortillas
	salsa, shredded lettuce, grated cheese

⊷ Cut steak into long strips and place in a covered dish. Combine oil, vinegar, onions, honey, soy sauce, ginger and garlic powder in a jar and shake. Pour over steak, making sure all pieces of meat are submerged in marinade. Let stand 8 to 12 hours in refrigerator.

⊷ When ready to serve, cook meat strips about 3 minutes on each side over a bed of hot coals, or over high heat on a charcoal or gas grill. Meat will flame when first put on grill.

⊷ Warm tortillas and prepare bowls of salsa, lettuce and cheese. Place cooked meat in tortillas and top with garnishes. Enjoy!

Sour Cream Enchiladas

A great dish for a casual supper. Serve with a garden fresh salad and mugs of beer.

SERVES 6

MAKES 6 FLOUR TORTILLAS

Filling

1 lb	ground beef
1 ½	packages taco seasoning
1 ½ cups	water

Sauce

1 lb	jalapeno pepper processed cheese
¼ cup	butter
1	onion, chopped
2 cups	sour cream

❧ Brown meat, then add taco seasoning and water. Simmer meat while preparing the sauce.

❧ To make sauce, melt cheese and butter. Add onions and sour cream and stir well.

❧ Spoon meat filling in center of tortillas and roll up. Place side by side in a casserole dish. For variation, tortillas may be layered with the meat rather than rolling. Pour cheese sauce over top and bake in a 350° F oven until heated through.

Mexican Lasagna

SERVES 6 TO 8

1 lb	ground beef
¼ cup	taco seasoning
10	10-inch flour tortillas
1	14 oz can refried beans
2 cups	Jack or mozzarella cheese, grated
1 cup	salsa
½ cup	green pepper, chopped
¾ cup	taco sauce

❧ In a frying pan, cook beef until browned and stir in taco seasoning.

❧ Spray a 10-inch springform pan with nonstick cooking spray. Place 2 tortillas in bottom of pan. Cover with half the meat mixture. Cover meat with 2 more tortillas. Add refried beans and 1 cup of cheese.

❧ Layer 2 tortillas on top of beans and cheese. Cover with salsa and green pepper. Layer with 2 more tortillas and cover with remaining meat mixture.

❧ Place last 2 tortillas in pan. Cover with taco sauce and remaining cup of cheese.

❧ Cover with foil and bake at 350° F for 45 minutes. Remove from oven and run a knife around edge before removing pan collar. Cut into wedges and serve with guacamole.

Mexican Quiche

A Southwest twist on a traditional French dish. Serve with a green salad and white wine.

SERVES 6

12	slices bacon, cooked crisp, crumbled
1 ½ cups	sharp Cheddar cheese, grated
½ cup	onion, minced
⅓ cup	green pepper, finely chopped
4	eggs
2 cups	light cream
¾ tsp	salt
¼ tsp	sugar
⅛ tsp	chili powder
1	unbaked single-crust pie shell

❧ Cook bacon well, drain and crumble. Sprinkle bacon, cheese, onion and green pepper in pastry-lined pie plate.

❧ Beat eggs slightly, then beat in remaining ingredients. Pour mixture into pie shell.

❧ Bake 15 minutes in a 425° F oven, then reduce temperature to 300° F and bake 30 minutes longer, or until knife inserted in center comes out clean. Let stand 10 minutes before cutting.

Chimichangas de Frijoles y Queso

Chimichangas are an Arizona specialty.

SERVES 8

2 tbsp	oil
2	16 oz cans refried beans
¼ cup	onion, diced
1	4 oz can green chiles
1 cup	Longhorn cheese, grated (may substitute Jack cheese)
8	flour tortillas
	lettuce, salsa, cheese for garnish

ᨀ Heat oil in a frying pan and add beans, onion, green chiles and small amount of water. Heat, stirring frequently, until warmed through. Blend in cheese and stir until melted.

ᨀ To fill tortillas, add ½ cup bean mixture to one end and fold top and bottom edges over to cover part of filling. Fold over other end and roll up. Repeat for remaining tortillas.

ᨀ Heat oil in a frying pan and cook chimichangas, seam-side down, then turn over and cook other side. Fry one at a time until golden brown. Garnish with lettuce, salsa and cheese.

Huevos Rancheros

Add tomato, onions and chile to eggs and you have what is commonly called ranch-style eggs, a favorite not only in the Southwest but as far north as a cowboy can ride.

SERVES 6

6	corn tortillas
6 tbsp	oil
6	eggs
¼ cup	melted butter
½ cup	cheese, grated

❧ Fry the corn tortillas in hot oil for 30 seconds, or until soft. Drain tortillas on paper towels and place on warm plates.

❧ Gently fry eggs, one at a time, in melted butter. Place a warm tortilla on each plate and put fried egg on top. Cover with green chile and tomato sauce (recipe next page). Top with cheese and serve immediately.

Green Chile and Tomato Sauce

2 tbsp	oil
½ cup	onion, chopped
1	14 oz can tomatoes, drained, diced
1	fresh jalapeno pepper, thinly sliced
	salt to taste

🖛 Heat oil and sauté onion for 1 minute. Do not allow to brown. Add tomatoes, salt and jalapeno slices. Cook 3 minutes, or until flavors blend. Remove from heat and serve over eggs.

Gorditas

This is a great dish for breakfast, lunch or dinner!

SERVES 10

12	4-inch corn tortillas
8	eggs, beaten
¼ cup	oil
1 cup	chorizo sausage, coarsely chopped
3	jalapeno peppers, coarsely chopped
	cilantro and salsa for garnish

&. Cut tortillas in half. Stack and wrap together in foil. Warm in 325° F oven for about 10 minutes. The tortillas should open like pockets.

&. While tortillas are warming, scramble eggs in oil. Heat sausage in small amount of oil in a separate frying pan. When eggs are done, combine with sausage and remaining ingredients in a bowl. Fill tortilla pockets with egg-sausage mixture and serve. Garnish with fresh cilantro and salsa.

[Snacks & Desserts]

Pecan Drops

These are melt-in-your-mouth delicious.

Makes 2 ½ dozen cookies

½ cup	butter
6 tbsp	white sugar
6 tbsp	brown sugar
1	egg
½ tsp	vanilla
1 ¼ cups	flour, sifted
1 tsp	baking powder
¼ tsp	baking soda
¼ tsp	salt
1 cup	pecans, chopped

⋅ Cream butter and sugars. Add egg and vanilla and beat well. In a separate bowl, combine flour, baking powder, baking soda and salt. Add to creamed mixture and mix well. Add pecans. Drop by teaspoonfuls onto ungreased cookie sheets. Bake about 10 minutes at 350° F. Cool slightly before removing from pan.

Bisochitos

The anise seed that gives bisochitos their distinctive taste was introduced in the early 1800s by Spanish priests when they came to New Mexico via Mexico's Chihuahua Trail.

MAKES 4 DOZEN COOKIES

¼ cup	sugar
1 tsp	ground cinnamon
1 cup	butter
3 cups	flour
1 tsp	anise seed, toasted
1 tsp	vanilla
1	egg
1 cup	sugar
¼ cup	brandy
1 ½ tsp	baking powder
½ tsp	salt

❧ Combine sugar and cinnamon and set aside.

❧ Beat butter until soft. Add half the flour. Blend in anise, vanilla, egg, sugar, brandy, baking powder and salt. Beat until smooth. Add remaining flour. Divide dough in half, cover and chill.

❧ Roll out dough on a floured surface and cut into shapes. Place on ungreased cookie sheets and sprinkle with cinnamon-sugar mixture. Bake for 12 to 15 minutes in a 350° F oven.

Mango Ice Cream

A Southwest favorite and a cool way to end a hot, spicy meal.

SERVES 6 TO 8

1 ½ cups	milk
1 ½ cups	heavy cream
1 cup	sugar
9	egg yolks
2	ripe mangos, peeled and sliced

❧ In a medium heavy-bottomed saucepan, combine milk, cream and 1 tablespoon of sugar. Bring just to a scald.

❧ In a separate bowl, combine remaining sugar and egg yolks. Whisk just to blend. While gently whisking yolks, slowly add hot cream mixture. Return egg yolk-cream mixture to saucepan over medium-low heat. Cook, stirring constantly to prevent sticking, until mixture coats the back of a spoon.

❧ Strain into a bowl and set the bowl in another bowl filled with ice. Cool, stirring occasionally.

❧ Puree the mangoes in a food processor. Whisk the mango puree into the cooled custard. Put into an ice cream maker and freeze according to directions. When process is complete, transfer ice cream to a storage container and place in freezer until firm.

Mrs. Glen's Peach Cobbler

Mary Martin
Dry Creek Ranch, Spur, Texas

SERVES 4 TO 6

5 cups	fresh peaches, peeled, sliced
1 cup	sugar
	dash of salt
2 tbsp	cornstarch
½ tsp	vanilla
½ cup	half and half cream
1 tsp	ground cinnamon
2 tbsp	butter
1	unbaked single-crust pie shell

❧ To peel peaches dip in boiling water for about 20 seconds. Remove with a slotted spoon and rinse under cold water. Peel and pit peaches, then cut into slices.

❧ In a large saucepan, heat sliced peaches with salt and ¾ cup sugar until bubbles form around edge of pan. Mix together remaining sugar, cornstarch, vanilla, cream and cinnamon. Slowly add mixture to peaches, stirring constantly until thickened. Stir in butter.

❧ Pour in warmed Dutch oven. Cover with favorite pie crust, sprinkle with sugar and dot with butter. Cover with preheated Dutch oven lid. Add coals to lid and cook until crust is golden brown.

Pecan Pie

Emily Permenter
Brownwood, Texas

No discussion of Texas cuisine would be complete without paying homage to the pecan tree and the delicious fruit it bears.

SERVES 6

3 tbsp	flour
1 cup	sugar
1 cup	white syrup
½ cup	evaporated milk
¼ tsp	vanilla
2	eggs
1 cup	pecans, chopped
1	unbaked single-crust pie shell

❧ Mix flour and sugar well. Add syrup, milk, vanilla and slightly beaten eggs. Pour into unbaked pie shell. Sprinkle chopped pecans over filling. Bake at 350° F for 45 to 60 minutes.

Grasshopper Pie

Fortunately, grasshopper pie bears no resemblance to its name. The creme de menthe lends a cool flavor to this delicious Southern dessert.

SERVES 6

1	16 oz package Oreo cookies
¼ cup	melted butter
1 bag	white marshmallows
1 cup	milk
2 cups	cream, whipped
6 tbsp	creme de menthe liqueur

❧ Crush cookies into fine crumbs, reserving a few crumbs for topping. Add melted butter to remaining crumbs and mix well. Press mixture into a 9 x 13-inch pan or two pie plates.

❧ Using a double boiler, melt marshmallows in milk. Set aside to cool. Mixture will become syrupy as it cools.

❧ Add whipped cream when marshmallow mixture is cool. Fold in creme de menthe. Pour over crust and top with reserved crumbs. Refrigerate overnight. Can also be frozen.

Dirt Dessert

An interesting and unique way to serve dessert. Dirt dessert is found in restaurants from Texas to Canada.

1	16 oz package Oreo cookies
1	8 oz package cream cheese
¾ cup	butter
1 cup	sugar
8 oz	Cool Whip
2	3 oz packages instant chocolate pudding
2 ½ cups	milk
½ cup	Irish Cream liqueur
	flower pot, 6 ½-inches in diameter by 5-inches high
	washed fresh flowers

❧ Crush cookies in blender or food processor and set aside. Mix together cream cheese, butter, sugar and Cool Whip. In another bowl, mix chocolate pudding, milk and Irish Cream liqueur. Stir cream cheese and pudding mixtures together.

❧ Line bottom of flower pot with aluminum foil. Spread half the cookie crumbs on bottom. Pour in pudding mixture. Top with remaining cookie crumbs. Refrigerate until ready to serve. Just before serving, insert flowers into pot. To serve, spoon into individual dessert dishes.

Black Forest Cheesecake

The Germans who immigrated to Texas after the Spaniards arrived brought their unique cuisine with them. Here is a variation of a well-known German dessert.

1 ¼ cup	chocolate wafers, crushed
⅓ cup	melted butter
2	envelopes unflavored gelatin
4 tbsp	hot water
1	19 oz can cherry pie filling
1 tsp	almond extract
2	8 oz packages cream cheese, softened
⅓ cup	white sugar
3 oz	semisweet chocolate, melted
2 tbsp	cherry brandy
1 cup	sour cream
1 pint	whipping cream
2 tbsp	icing sugar
	semisweet chocolate, grated cherries for garnish

ა Combine chocolate wafers and melted butter. Press into springform pan and chill.

ა Dissolve one envelope of gelatin in 2 tablespoons of hot water. Add to cherry pie filling and mix in almond extract. Pour over wafer crust and chill.

ა Beat cream cheese and sugar together. Beat in melted chocolate. Add brandy and sour cream.

❧ Dissolve second envelope of gelatin in 2 tablespoons of hot water and add to cream cheese mixture. Pour over pie filling mixture and chill again.

❧ Whip cream with icing sugar and cover top of cheesecake. Decorate with grated chocolate and cherries. Chill until serving.

Lemon Meringue Bread Pudding

The tart flavor of lemon curd is the perfect ending to a spicy South-west meal. Placing it on top of a moist slice of torejas turns it into a homestyle bread pudding.

SERVES 6

Lemon Curd

1 tbsp	cornstarch
½ cup	heavy cream
2	eggs
4	egg yolks
	grated zest of 1 lemon
¾ cup	fresh lemon juice
½ cup	fresh orange juice
¾ cup	sugar
½ tsp	vanilla extract
4 tbsp	unsalted butter

Meringue

4	egg whites
½ cup	sugar
¼ tsp	salt
	pinch of cream of tartar

&. First make the lemon curd. Whisk cornstarch and cream together in a medium bowl. Whisk in eggs and egg yolks. Set aside.

&. In a medium saucepan, combine zest, fruit juices, sugar, vanilla and butter and bring to a boil over medium heat.

Whisking constantly, slowly drizzle half the hot liquid into the cream mixture. Return everything to the saucepan and cook, whisking constantly and scraping the bottom of the pan, until tiny bubbles boil up for 10 seconds. Strain the curd through a fine sieve into a bowl, cover and set aside. The curd can be prepared a day ahead and refrigerated.

❧ When ready to serve, prepare torejas (recipe next page) and make meringue.

❧ To make meringue, place egg whites, sugar, salt and cream of tartar in a large stainless steel bowl and set over a pan of simmering water. Whisk until mixture is lukewarm. Remove from heat and beat until egg whites form stiff peaks.

❧ Spread lemon curd over still warm torejas. Pile meringue on top of curd. Set pudding under a preheated broiler for a few seconds, until meringue is nicely browned. May be stored up to 24 hours in the refrigerator.

Torejas

SERVES 6

6	slices brioche or challah bread
½ cup	milk
½ cup	heavy cream
2 tbsp	sugar
2	eggs
2	egg yolks
1 tsp	vanilla
1 tbsp	dark rum (optional)
1 tsp	ground cinnamon (optional)
½ cup	ground nutmeg (optional)

ᕲ Prepare the bread a day in advance by trimming crusts and cutting into ¾-inch thick slices. Lay bread out on a cookie sheet to dry.

ᕲ When ready to cook, preheat oven to 375° F and set the rack in the middle of the oven. Lightly grease a cookie sheet.

ᕲ In a medium bowl, whisk remaining ingredients. Omit optional ingredients if using bread with lemon curd and meringue. Dip slices of bread in the mixture and soak well, about 5 minutes, then turn and soak the other side. Shake off excess mixture and place on cookie sheet.

ᕲ Bake for 12 minutes, or until golden and crusty on the top but still moist and custardlike inside. Serve warm with lemon curd and meringue or with ice cream.

[Beverages]

Morning Eye-Popper

This breakfast drink is an invigorating way to start the day. Add vodka and you've got a late afternoon refresher.

SERVES 6

1	14 oz can V-8 juice
1	6 oz can tomato sauce
2 cups	orange juice
1 dash	Tabasco sauce
⅓ cup	freshly squeezed lemon juice
1 tsp	celery salt
1 tsp	onion salt or powder
2 tbsp	Worcestershire sauce
	vodka (optional)

🍃 Mix all ingredients and serve over ice.

Mexican Hot Chocolate

In Aztec society chocolate was reserved for the noble classes who used it as a potent ceremonial drink.

SERVES 4

3 cups	milk
¼ cup	sugar
1 ½ oz	unsweetened chocolate, chopped
½ tsp	ground cinnamon
1	egg, beaten
1 tsp	vanilla
	whipped cream

In a saucepan, combine 1 cup of milk with sugar, chocolate and cinnamon. Cook slowly until chocolate is melted, stirring constantly. Stir in remaining milk and heat until very hot but not boiling.

Carefully stir ½ cup hot milk mixture into egg. Transfer egg mixture back to saucepan. Cook and stir over low heat for 2 minutes. Remove and add vanilla, beating until frothy. Serve in mugs topped with whipped cream.

Orange Milk Punch

A frothy, refreshing concoction that starts any day well. Also great on hot summer afternoons.

SERVES 6

1	6 oz can frozen orange juice concentrate
1 cup	milk
1 cup	water
¼ cup	white sugar
2	eggs (optional)
10 to 12	ice cubes

❧ Combine ingredients in a blender and process until smooth and foamy. Serve immediately while still frothy.

Pineapple Fruit Cocktail

This is a refreshing blend of fruit juices and ginger ale for hot summer days.

SERVES 8 TO 10

1	12 oz can frozen orange juice concentrate
1	12 oz can frozen lemonade concentrate
4 cups	pineapple juice
1	2 quart bottle ginger ale (optional)
	ice cubes (optional)
	fruit slices for garnish

❧ Mix concentrates and pineapple juice together. Add ginger ale and ice, if desired. Garnish with fruit slices. For variation, try using 32 ounces each of white wine and 7-Up instead of ginger ale.

Summer Punch

A cool drink for Sunday brunch. Double or triple the recipe for company.

SERVES 2

2	large peaches, peeled and sliced
¾ cup	vodka
2 tbsp	icing sugar
	crushed ice
1	12 oz can frozen lemonade concentrate
	strawberries or mint leaf for garnish

❧ To peel peaches dip in boiling water for about 20 seconds. Remove with a slotted spoon and rinse under cold water. Peel and pit peaches, then cut into slices. Place peaches and remaining ingredients in a blender and process until mixture is smooth. Pour into chilled glasses and garnish with a strawberry or mint leaf.

Mint Juleps

A real Southern treat, this classic cocktail is the official drink of the Kentucky Derby.

SERVES 6 TO 8

2 cups	sugar
1 cup	water
10	sprigs of mint
	bourbon
	crushed ice

❧ Combine sugar and water and boil for 5 minutes. Add the leaves from sprigs of mint. Let mixture sit for 12 hours, or until it forms a syrup.

❧ Add 2 jiggers bourbon to 1 jigger of syrup. Pour over crushed ice and garnish with mint leaves.

Frozen Daiquiris

Daiquiris are an excellent choice for a large gathering. They can be made well ahead of time and appeal to most folks.

SERVES 20 OR MORE

2	12 oz cans frozen lemonade concentrate
2	12 oz cans frozen limeade concentrate
1 quart	light rum
8 cups	water

🍂 Blend all ingredients together and store in freezer. Remove from freezer as needed. Let mixture turn slushy and spoon into glasses.

Margaritas

You will need a cocktail shaker to whip up these margaritas to go with your favorite Mexican appetizer.

SERVES 1

	lime
	coarse salt
	crushed ice
½ oz	triple sec
1 ½ oz	tequila

❧ Rub the cut side of a lime around the rim of a 10-ounce cocktail glass, then dip the rim into a plate of coarse salt. Pack the glass with crushed ice. Set aside.

❧ Into a shaker full of ice, squeeze juice of half a lime. Use your fingers to give a good squeeze as this will get some of the oil from the skin of the lime into the margarita.

❧ Add ½ ounce of triple sec and 1 ½ ounces of good tequila. Shake until thoroughly chilled and strain into the salted glass.

The Great Plains &
The Northern Ranges

Colorado, Kansas, Nebraska, Oklahoma, Utah, Wyoming, Idaho, Montana, North Dakota, South Dakota

WHILE THE AMERICAN GREAT PLAINS IS HOME TO many different cultures and religions, there is a unifying culinary feature evident in most of the region's kitchens. It is the no-nonsense approach to cooking that reflects an attitude born of people whose first concern was the taming of harsh land. Here the emphasis is less on exotic food and more on stick-to-the-ribs fare like beans and beef, food initially designed to get hard-working pioneers through a day behind an ox-drawn plow or a band saw.

The influences aren't as strongly Indian-based as is the case farther south, although the native people's contribution to the region's cuisine is still evident. These Native Americans relied far more on rice than corn and that influence certainly is present. But it was the rugged European settlers—Scandinavians, Germans, Swiss, Dutch, Amish and Mennonites—whose influence on the kitchens of the Midwest is still very much in evidence. And while the cuisine of the Great Plains states (Colorado, Kansas, Nebraska, Oklahoma, Utah and Wyoming) may lack the flair associated with chiles and tortillas, it is as interesting and enjoyable as any on the continent.

Travel north and you encounter a cuisine likewise rooted in the pragmatic. The cattle came late to the north country and so did the settlers. When they arrived, they found a land with streams of sweet, clear water and grass-covered plains punctuated by mountains standing like sentinels guarding all that lay below. Though very different from the Great Plains, the magnificent landscape of the Northern Range nevertheless provided endless obstacles to overcome. And food was scarce. Out of necessity, the earliest pioneers found ways to co-exist with the often inhospitable terrain. They quickly learned to take what the land would give. The hunter able to bring down deer, elk or bear could feed his family for long periods.

Eventually, with the arrival of the railroad and better food supplies, ranch life on the Northern Range eased. Today, no single cuisine is the trademark of the area, but the food remains faithful to a rugged heritage. Take a rainbow trout sizzling in a pan, some new Idaho potatoes, venison stew cooking up in a Dutch oven or pancakes served under a mound of freshly picked huckleberries and you're likely to have a pretty good sampling of the food found on the ranches of Idaho, Montana and the Dakotas.

[Starters]

Spinach-in-a-Loaf

Popular at any community gathering, this dip is as impressive as it is easy to prepare.

SERVES 6 TO 8

1	round loaf of bread
2	8 oz packages cream cheese
1 cup	Cheddar cheese, grated
2 tsp	dill weed
1 cup	mayonnaise
¼ cup	onion, diced
½ cup	bacon bits
1	7 oz can crab meat, drained
1	package frozen spinach, thawed, drained, chopped

❧ Hollow out the loaf. Cube the bread and reserve until serving time. Mix remaining ingredients, adding the spinach last. Put the spinach mixture inside the hollow loaf, wrap in foil and bake at 325° F for 1 hour. Serve hot with cubed bread for dipping.

Salmon Ball

A tasty appetizer to snack on before dinner.

SERVES 8 TO 10

1 cup	canned salmon
1	8 oz package cream cheese
1 tbsp	lemon juice
1 tbsp	onion, grated
2 to 3 tbsp	horseradish
¼ tsp	salt
¼ tsp	hot pepper sauce
¼ tsp	Worcestershire sauce
	chopped nuts
	parsley

🔊 Warm cream cheese to room temperature. Drain salmon well and mix with cream cheese and remaining ingredients except nuts and parsley. Chill well. Form into two small balls or one large ball and roll in chopped nuts and parsley. Chill again. Serve with crackers.

Buckaroo Crackers

When you want something to munch on, try these crackers.

MAKES 12 CRACKERS

¼ lb	butter
½ lb	Cheddar cheese, grated
½	package onion soup mix
½ tsp	salt
1 cup	flour

🍃 Butter and cheese should be at room temperature. Mix together until well blended. Add remaining ingredients and mix. Shape into 1-inch logs, wrap in wax paper and chill.

🍃 When ready to bake, slice into ¼-inch thick rounds. Bake on an ungreased cookie sheet at 375° F for 10 to 12 minutes, or until slightly brown. Do not overbake.

[Breads]

Carol's Oklahoma Cornbread

Carol Toole
Mangum, Oklahoma

Carol is the wife of former Professional Rodeo Cowboy Association Bullrider Gary Toole and sister of Canadian All-Around and Bareback Champion Steve Dunham. She has seen her share of rodeos and fed lots of hungry cowboys.

SERVES 6

1 cup	cornmeal
1	16 oz can cream-style corn
¾ cup	milk
½ tsp	baking soda
⅓ cup	butter, melted
1 tsp	salt
2	eggs, lightly beaten
2 cups	sharp Cheddar cheese, grated
1	4 oz can green chiles, diced

❧ Preheat oven to 400° F. Combine all ingredients in a large bowl and mix well. Pour into a greased 9 x 9-inch baking pan. Bake 30 minutes. Serve with baked beans, stew or chili.

Johnnycake

An early pioneer favorite, Johnnycake is popular both as a bread accompaniment to a meal or as a dessert with maple syrup.

SERVES 8

1 ½ cups	flour
1 tsp	baking powder
½ tsp	salt
½ cup	sugar
1 ½ cups	cornmeal
1 ¾ cups	sour milk
1 tsp	baking soda
1	egg, beaten
½ cup	corn kernels
3 tbsp	melted butter

🍂 Mix dry ingredients in a bowl. Make a well and add sour milk mixed with baking soda and egg. Stir in corn kernels and butter last. Pour into greased pan and bake at 375° F for 40 to 45 minutes, or until toothpick inserted in the center comes out clean.

Sourdough Pancakes

These pancakes are just the thing for a hearty breakfast at home or out on the trail. Serve with butter and syrup.

MAKES 12 PANCAKES

1 cup	sourdough starter (recipe page 33)
1 ½ cups	flour
2 tbsp	sugar
1 tsp	baking powder
½ tsp	baking soda
½ tsp	salt
2	eggs, beaten
3 tbsp	melted shortening

❧ Bring sourdough starter to room temperature before using.

❧ Combine flour, sugar, baking powder, baking soda and salt. In a separate bowl, mix sourdough starter, eggs and shortening. Combine the two mixtures, stirring until just blended. Pour batter onto a preheated, greased griddle and cook until pancakes are brown, turning once.

Berry Muffins

Prepare these delicious muffins with either fresh or frozen berries.

MAKES 12 TO 18 MUFFINS

⅔ cup	sugar
⅓ cup	butter
2	eggs, well beaten
2 cups	flour
2 tsp	baking powder
½ tsp	salt
⅔ cup	milk
1 ½ cups	assorted berries

⫐ These muffins can be made with huckleberries (may substitute blueberries), raspberries, blackberries or a mixture of all.

⫐ Cream butter and sugar. Add eggs. Sift dry ingredients and add alternately with milk to creamed ingredients. Fold in berries. Bake in greased muffin tins at 375° F for 20 minutes, or until lightly browned.

Sourdough Banana-Cherry Bread

This is a rich, moist loaf that keeps well. Serve with fresh-perked coffee when company comes!

SERVES 12

1 cup	sourdough starter (recipe page 33)
1 cup	sugar
½ cup	butter
2	eggs
1 cup	flour
1 tsp	baking soda
½ tsp	vanilla
2	large ripe bananas, mashed
¾ cup	maraschino cherries, drained and chopped
1 cup	milk chocolate chips

❧ Bring sourdough starter to room temperature before using.

❧ Cream sugar, butter and eggs. Add sourdough starter and stir. Add remaining ingredients, blending well. Bake in a greased loaf pan or 9 x 9-inch cake pan for 50 to 60 minutes at 350° F, or until toothpick inserted in center comes out clean.

Cheese-Apple Bread

A moist, flavorful loaf that adds flare to any lunchbox or tea.

SERVES 12

½ cup	butter
2	eggs
1 ½ tsp	baking powder
½ tsp	baking soda
1 tsp	salt
1 cup	apples, peeled, grated
½ cup	Cheddar cheese, grated
⅔ cup	sugar
2 cups	flour

❧ Combine butter, eggs and dry ingredients in a bowl, mixing well. Fold in apples and cheese. Place in a well-greased 9 x 5-inch loaf pan. Bake at 350° F for about 1 hour. Cool before removing from pan and serve with butter.

[Salads & Side Dishes]

Ranch Cole Slaw

Jeannine Lahrman
Tarryall River Ranch, Lake George, Colorado

Cole slaw is a great addition to any meal. The word comes from the Dutch cool for cabbage (Kohl in German) and sla for salad.

SERVES 10 TO 12

½ cup	half and half cream
¼ cup	sugar
3 tbsp	apple cider vinegar
1 tbsp	mayonnaise
1	clove garlic, minced
½ tsp	salt
1	small head white cabbage, grated
⅛	head purple cabbage, grated
1 to 2	carrots, peeled, grated
¼ cup	pineapple, diced

❧ Mix cream, sugar, vinegar, mayonnaise, garlic and salt together. Blend well. Add cabbage, carrots and pineapple and mix well. Chill for 1 hour. The longer you chill this salad, the better it tastes!

Crunchy Cabbage Salad

Gail Lander
Kedesh Ranch, Shell, Wyoming

This salad is a big favorite. It's popular as a holiday side dish or served up at summer cookouts.

SERVES 4

2 tbsp	sugar
3 tbsp	vinegar
⅓ to ½ cup	oil
½ tsp	pepper
1	3 oz package oriental-style noodles (with flavor packet)
½	large head of cabbage, grated
4	green onions, chopped
2 tbsp	sesame seeds
½ cup	slivered almonds

❧ Mix sugar, vinegar, oil, pepper and packet from noodle mix early in the day and refrigerate.

❧ Break uncooked noodles into pieces. Combine with grated cabbage and onions. Just before serving, add dressing and toss lightly. Sprinkle seeds and nuts over top and toss again. Serve immediately.

Range Rider Layered Salad

A handy salad to serve when you have to take a meal to the branding corrals or the hayfield. It can be made the day before to save time. While there are variations on this salad, most layered salads include peas and cheese.

SERVES 12

2	large heads of lettuce, shredded
1 lb	package frozen peas
1	green bell pepper, chopped
1 cup	celery, chopped
½ lb	bacon, cooked crisp, crumbled
1	Spanish onion, chopped
	freshly ground pepper
1 cup	mayonnaise
2 tbsp	sugar
1 cup	Parmesan cheese

≈ Fill a large salad bowl half full with shredded lettuce. Layer peas, green pepper, celery and bacon. Layer the onion on top and add freshly ground pepper. Add another layer of lettuce.

≈ Mix mayonnaise and sugar and frost the top, making sure to cover all the lettuce as this will keep the salad crisp. Sprinkle the top with Parmesan cheese and store overnight in the refrigerator to allow flavors to blend.

Twenty-Four-Hour Omelet

Buck and Sandra Bailey
Breeze Hill Ranch, Chandler, Oklahoma

This recipe is a company dish at Breeze Hill Ranch. It's a great dish that can be made ahead to save time.

SERVES 6 TO 8

5	slices white sandwich breads
	butter
¾ lb	Cheddar cheese, grated
4	eggs, beaten
2 cups	milk
½ tsp	dry mustard
½ tsp	salt
	dash of cayenne pepper

❧ Trim crusts and butter one side of each slice of bread. Cut bread into 1-inch cubes. Place cubes evenly in a well-buttered 9 x 9-inch casserole dish. Sprinkle bread with cheese. Mix eggs, milk, mustard, salt and pepper and pour over bread. Refrigerate, covered, overnight. The next morning bake in 350° F oven for about 1 hour, or until egg mixture is set. Uncover for the last 5 minutes.

Hash Brown Casserole

Virginia Purdy
Purdy Ranch, Buffalo, Wyoming

This dish is ideal for busy cooks. It can be made ahead and baked when needed.

SERVES 4 TO 6

1	package frozen hash brown potatoes
2 cups	sour cream
1	10 oz can cream of chicken soup
½ cup	melted butter
½ cup	onion, grated
	salt and pepper to taste
2 cups	sharp Cheddar cheese, grated

❧ Layer frozen hash brown potatoes in a casserole dish. Mix sour cream, chicken soup, melted butter, onion and salt and pepper. Pour over potatoes and cover with grated cheese. Bake 1 hour at 325° to 350° F. Do not overbake. This dish can be made a day ahead and baked when needed.

New Potatoes

Idaho is famous for its potatoes and rightly so. The state overtook Maine in potato production after World War II, and today five hundred square miles of the state is planted in potatoes. This recipe is a great way to serve new potatoes. Serve it for breakfast or dinner!

SERVES 4 TO 6

4 tbsp	olive oil
5	large potatoes, peeled, diced
2	cloves garlic, minced
3 tbsp	green onion, finely chopped
2 tbsp	parsley, chopped
	salt and pepper to taste

❧ Heat olive oil in a large frying pan. Add potatoes and garlic to pan, cover and simmer over medium heat for 15 minutes, stirring occasionally. Uncover. Add onion, parsley and salt and pepper. Stir-fry for about 10 minutes, or until potatoes are tender.

Bunkhouse Potatoes

A delightful way to serve new potatoes.

SERVES 6

8 to 12	small red-skinned new potatoes
2 tbsp	butter
1	medium onion, finely chopped
4	green onions, cut in 1-inch pieces
2	large tomatoes, diced
½ cup	evaporated milk
1 tbsp	fresh cilantro, finely chopped
1 tbsp	oregano
½ tsp	cumin
	salt and pepper to taste
1 cup	mozzarella cheese, grated

❧ Scrub potatoes. Do not peel. Place potatoes in a large pot and cover with water. Boil, covered, until tender when pierced, about 20 minutes. Drain.

❧ Melt butter in a frying pan over medium heat. Add chopped onion and green onion. Cook until limp. Add tomatoes and cook, stirring often, for 5 minutes. Add milk, cilantro, oregano, cumin, salt and pepper. While stirring, slowly add cheese. Cook until melted. Serve at once spooned over hot potatoes.

Wild Rice Casserole

Virginia Purdy
Purdy Ranch, Buffalo, Wyoming

Deer hunting season lures the Purdy's Minnesota friends to Wyoming. They always bring some of their great wild rice for Virginia to cook.

Wild rice is actually not rice at all but the grainlike seed of grass that grows in shallow lake waters in north-central United States and parts of southern Canada. Wild rice was a staple in the diets of early Native Americans.

SERVES 4

1 cup	wild rice
1	10 oz can condensed consommé
1 tbsp	butter
½ lb	fresh mushrooms
	salt and pepper to taste

✌ Wash rice carefully. Place in a shallow casserole dish and cover with consommé. Let stand 3 hours, then bake, covered, in a 350° F oven for about 45 minutes, adding water if rice seems dry.

✌ Sauté mushrooms in butter and add to rice. Mix lightly with a fork. No crust should form, yet all liquid should be absorbed. This is a delicious supper dish with beef.

Cowboy Corn

A delightfully different way to serve canned corn.

SERVES 8

8	slices bacon, diced
8	scallions including tops, thinly sliced
2 tbsp	fresh dill, minced
½ tsp	salt
¼ tsp	pepper
3	14 oz cans whole kernel corn

❧ Brown bacon slowly. When cooked, pour off all but 2 tablespoons bacon drippings. Add scallions and sauté for 5 minutes. Add seasonings and sauté another 5 minutes, stirring occasionally. Drain corn and add to bacon mixture. Simmer until thoroughly heated.

High-Noon Onion Casserole

The secret to this recipe is to use good black rye bread.

SERVES 8

8	large yellow onions, chopped
4 tbsp	butter
2	10 oz cans cream of mushroom soup
1 ½ lbs	Swiss cheese, grated
	rye bread slices, buttered

❧ Coarsely chop onions. Cook in melted butter in a covered frying pan until soft and transparent, about 20 minutes. Stir in mushroom soup and cheese. Place in a buttered casserole. Top with buttered bread slices. Bake at 350° F for about 30 minutes.

[Main Dishes]

1880 Town and Longhorn Ranch Chili

Anna Marie Hullinger
1880 Town Longhorns, Murdo, South Dakota

Anna Marie has used this recipe for over thirty years. It was first served at the family's Tee Pee Restaurant and later in the Santa Fe dining cars at 1880 Town. 1880 Town and Longhorn Ranch, located twenty-two miles west of Murdo, South Dakota, is an authentic replica of a vintage Western town.

SERVES 20

4 lbs	ground beef
2	large onions, grated
4 cups	chili sauce
4 tbsp	chili powder
4 tbsp	brown sugar
1	48 oz can tomato juice
1	14 oz can chili beans in gravy
	salt and pepper to taste

&. Brown ground beef and onions. Add remaining ingredients except beans. Simmer 10 minutes. Add beans, heat thoroughly and serve.

Three B's Chili

Kathy Burrows
Three B's of Colorado, Greeley, Colorado

A combination of chiles and chocolate imparts a rich, robust flavor.

SERVES 8 TO 12

Mole

4	dry New Mexico chiles
4	dry Pasilla chiles
6 cups	water
4 oz	double bitter chocolate

Chili

3 oz	pure olive oil
2 lbs	top sirloin, cut into ½-inch cubes
½ lb	red bell pepper, diced
½ lb	green bell pepper, diced
½ lb	red onion, diced
2 tsp	fresh garlic, minced
1 tsp	black pepper, freshly ground
1 tsp	fresh oregano leaves, chopped
1 tsp	cumin
3 cups	beef stock, consommé or bouillon
	salt to taste
2	grilled sweet corn on cob

❧ Combine chiles, water and chocolate and bring to a boil. Reduce heat and simmer until water is reduced by half. Puree in a blender to make a base known as the mole. Set aside.

In separate pan, heat olive oil and sauté sirloin and vegetables. Add garlic and seasonings. Add beef stock and bring to a boil. Reduce heat to a simmer and stir in the mole. Simmer slowly to meld flavors and adjust seasoning as needed. Grilled sweet corn should be folded in at the very end.

Buffalo-Sausage Red Chili

George E. Carlberg C.E.C.
Buckhorn Exchange Restaurant, Denver, Colorado

*This recipe was first place winner at the Mile Hi Chili Cookoff for
1991 and 1993. It's a good one.*

SERVES 6

1 lb	buffalo, chopped
1 lb	breakfast-style pork sausage
1 cup	water
½ cup	onion, diced
½ cup	celery, diced
1	green pepper, diced
¼ cup	red chile
2 tbsp	cumin
1 tbsp	salt
1 tbsp	sugar
1 tbsp	white pepper
3 tbsp	garlic powder
1	4 oz can green chile strips
1	14 oz can kidney beans
1	14 oz can pinto beans
1	28 oz can tomatoes, diced
2 tbsp	vinegar
1 tbsp	Worcestershire sauce
2 tsp	beef base
1 tsp	chicken base

&. Combine first 3 ingredients in a saucepan and cook until

meat is browned. Use potato masher to break up pieces of meat if necessary. Drain.

❧ Add next 10 ingredients and simmer for 15 minutes.

❧ Add remaining ingredients and bring to a boil. Add 1 to 2 cups of water to bring to desired consistency. Simmer 30 minutes.

Buffalo Red-Eye Stew

George E. Carlberg C.E.C.
Buckhorn Exchange Restaurant, Denver, Colorado

Before the turn of the century large herds of buffalo roamed the plains, and Native Americans and pioneers alike depended heavily on the meat for sustenance. Buffalo herds dwindled drastically, but conservation has seen their numbers grow over the past few years. Buffalo meat is tender and similar in taste to beef, although darker in color.

SERVES 6

4	potatoes
¼ lb	butter
2 lbs	buffalo stew meat (preferably sirloin)
½	yellow onion, diced
¼ tsp	white pepper
¼ tsp	leaf thyme
1 tsp	basil
½ tsp	salt
1 ½ tsp	garlic powder
½ cup	flour
2 cups	water
1	28 oz can tomatoes, diced
½ cup	bourbon
½ cup	strong coffee
1 tbsp	Worcestershire

❧ Peel potatoes and cut into 1-inch cubes. Place potatoes in a saucepan, cover with water and bring to a boil. Reduce heat to simmer and continue to cook until potatoes are about half done. Do not overcook.

ã In a large saucepan, melt butter over medium heat, add stew meat, onions and dry spices. Allow to simmer while potatoes are cooking. When potatoes are half done, add flour to buffalo meat. Mix well and cook for 5 minutes. Add tomatoes and simmer for 5 minutes.

ã Drain potatoes and add to stew along with remaining ingredients. Gently stir together. Return to a boil, reduce heat and allow to simmer for 30 minutes, or until buffalo is tender.

Mountain Man Stew

Montana's mountains were the scene of gold and silver prospecting during the gold rush days of the 1860s and the silver strikes of the 1880s. Fortunes were made and lost.

SERVES 6 TO 8

Trail Dust

½ cup	flour
1 ½ tsp	ground cloves
½ tsp	ground allspice
½ tsp	ground cinnamon
½ tsp	salt

Stew

3 ½ to 4 lbs	stewing beef, cubed
2 tbsp	shortening
1	10 oz can beef consommé
1 tbsp	sugar
4 oz	bourbon
3 to 4 cups	carrots, diced
3 to 4 cups	potatoes, diced
1	small onion
	beef broth or water

ᨒ Make trail dust by combining flour with spices. Dredge meat in seasoned flour and fry in hot shortening. Add consommé, sugar, bourbon, vegetables and remaining trail dust. Add water or beef broth to cover and cook on low heat for about 2 hours.

Montana Elk Steak

Montana is world renowned for its big game hunting. This recipe is a simple yet delicious way to prepare elk.

SERVES 2

½ tsp	salt
½ tsp	fresh black pepper, coarsely ground
½ cup	olive oil
2	6 oz elk steaks, boneless, ½-inch thick
1 cup	red wine

❧ Combine salt, pepper and oil. Mix until salt is dissolved. Using ¼ cup of the mixture, rub well on both sides of the steak. Let stand 15 minutes. Place steaks in a shallow casserole dish and add wine. Let stand 20 minutes, turning 2 or 3 times.

❧ Heat remaining oil mixture in a frying pan and cook steaks to desired doneness. Turn steaks once during cooking. During last 30 seconds of cooking, add remaining wine and cover.

Steak Casserole

Michelle Schulte
Rock'n Bar Ranch, Big Cabin, Oklahoma

This recipe is a great time-saver when you're busy. Simply place the ingredients in a crockpot or a casserole dish in the oven, and dinner will cook while you go about your chores.

SERVES 4 TO 5

1 ½ to 2 lbs	round steak
1	onion, minced
2 to 3	large potatoes, chopped
1 to 2	carrots, sliced
1	10 oz can tomato soup
1	10 oz can golden mushroom soup
1 tbsp	Worcestershire sauce
⅓ cup	water

ea Cube steak and place in bottom of a casserole dish. Add vegetables. Combine soups, Worcestershire sauce and water. Pour mixture over meat and vegetables. Bake, covered, for 2 hours in a 375° F oven. Serve over white rice.

Onion Steak Bake

Julie Saddler
Prairie Wind Ranch, Colby, Kansas

Julie Saddler uses this recipe a lot when they're calving at the ranch or during the winter when chores take up so much time. It's an easy recipe that requires little clean-up.

SERVES 5 TO 6

2 lbs	round or sirloin steak
1	package dry onion soup mix
4 tbsp	water
1	medium onion, sliced
	heavy duty foil

❧ Lay out foil. Place meat in center and sprinkle with onion soup mix, then drizzle with water. Place sliced onion on top. Fold foil over, sealing edges. Place on center rack in oven and bake at 350° F for 1 ½ to 2 hours, depending on the cut of meat (325° F for tougher cuts of meat). Julie throws baking potatoes into the oven halfway through cooking the steak for an easy supper.

Grandma Fanny's Pot Roast

George E. Carlberg C.E.C.
The Buckhorn Exchange Restaurant, Denver, Colorado

This popular dish has been on the menu since the 1940s.

SERVES 10 TO 12

1	5 lb beef brisket or shoulder roast
1 tbsp ea	paprika and pepper
1	large onion, chopped
1	stalk celery, chopped
1	large tomato, diced
2	carrots, chopped
	equal parts flour and butter
	salt, pepper, garlic, Worcestershire
	sauce to taste

☙ Heat a large cast iron Dutch oven over a high flame until the point at which droplets of water sizzle. Sear the brisket on both sides until evenly browned.

☙ Remove from heat, thoroughly coat meat with seasonings. Reduce heat. Add chopped vegetables, cover and return to the heat. Allow the roast to slow-cook on the stove top. Total cooking time will be about 4 hours.

☙ After 3 ½ hours, remove the lid and check for tenderness with a fork. If the meat is not tender, replace cover and continue to cook. When satisfied with the tenderness, remove the meat from the juices and place in a warm oven.

❧ Increase the heat under the Dutch oven and allow the juices to boil. Add equal parts flour and butter to thicken and whisk well. Return to a boil and season with salt, pepper, garlic and Worcestershire. Strain the finished sauce through a double mesh strainer. Serve ¼-inch slices of roast between slices of black rye bread with brown sauce drizzled over the meat.

Dutch Oven Dinner

Jean Kary
Reverse K Box Ranch, Norris, South Dakota

As is the case with many ranch cooks, Jean says she'd be lost without her cast iron Dutch oven, the same one her mother used for years.

SERVES 8

2 tbsp	oil
4 to 6 lb	chuck roast
½	package onion soup mix
1 to 2 quarts	water
10	potatoes
10	carrots
3	onions
4	stalks celery
½	large cabbage
	salt and pepper to taste

❧ Heat oil in Dutch oven, then brown meat on both sides. Place metal meat trivet in bottom of pot. Add chopped vegetables except cabbage. Season with salt and pepper. Add water, cover and place Dutch oven over hot coals or in 350° F oven. Bake for 1 ½ hours. During last half hour, add cabbage wedges. Replace lid and cook until vegetables are tender.

Ranch Tenderloin

Buck and Sandra Bailey
Breeze Hill Ranch, Chandler, Oklahoma

This beef recipe was given to the Baileys years ago by a good friend. They've shared it many times—everyone loves the great taste!

SERVES 6 TO 8

2 to 3 lbs	beef tenderloin
4 tbsp	soy sauce
2 tbsp	oil
1 tbsp	wine vinegar
1 tbsp	parsley
4	cloves garlic, minced
1 tsp	pepper
¼ tsp	ground ginger

Place meat in a large casserole dish. Mix remaining ingredients well, pour over meat and marinate overnight. Cook tenderloin at 450° F for 10 minutes, then at 350° F for about 30 minutes more, depending on how well done you like your beef. Double marinate recipe if cooking a larger cut of tenderloin.

Granny Fern's Barbecue Sauce

Victor and Stephanie Read
Read Ranch Inc., Chandler, Oklahoma

This recipe is a succulent accompaniment to almost any choice of barbecued meat at the popular Read Guest Ranch. The Ranch is just off historic Route 66, east of Oklahoma City.

MAKES 16 CUPS

1 gal	ketchup
1 ½ cups	vinegar
3 lbs	brown sugar
4 to 6 oz	prepared horseradish
1	10 oz bottle Worcestershire sauce
2 oz	liquid smoke
3 tbsp	dry mustard
2 tbsp	red pepper flakes
2 tbsp	salt

❧ Mix all ingredients together and heat until sugar dissolves. This barbecue sauce is a tasty accompaniment to baked beans or beef, pork, chicken or wild game dishes.

Barbecued Ribs 'n Grits

Cindy and Baxter Black
Coyote Cowboy Company, Brighton, Colorado

Cindy Black comments that the first time she and cowboy-poet hus-
band, Baxter, made this recipe, it was for a large crowd—the cast
and crew for a video in which Baxter was to be featured. The idea
was to cook these succulent Colorado ribs in a large fire pit. As luck
would have it, a strong wind, imported from Wyoming, blew in
and coated each delicious rib with pine needles and corral dust—
hence Ribs 'n Grits!

SERVES 6 TO 8

15	large country-style pork ribs
1 cup	ketchup
¼ cup	vinegar
3 tbsp	Worcestershire sauce
½ tsp	paprika
¾ cup	brown sugar
1 tsp	salt
¼ cup	lemon juice
1	5 oz can tomato paste
1 tbsp	mustard

❧ Place ribs in a single layer in a large casserole dish. Combine above ingredients and pour over ribs. Marinate ribs for a
few hours before cooking, or overnight. Barbecue over coals.

Oven-Barbecued Spareribs

Here's an easy oven-method for pork spareribs or beef ribs that begins with a marinade.

SERVES 4 TO 6

3 lbs	pork spareribs or beef ribs
1	onion, chopped
1	clove garlic, minced
½ cup	water
¼ cup	soy sauce
2 tbsp	Worcestershire sauce
1 tbsp	white wine or cider vinegar
½ tsp ea	dry mustard and ground ginger
	pinch pepper
2 tbsp	oil
	several splashes red pepper sauce

❧ Pat ribs dry and cut into serving-size pieces. Place ribs in a single layer in a large shallow casserole dish. Strew onions and garlic over ribs. Combine remaining ingredients in a jar and shake. Pour over meat. Cover and refrigerate at least 4 hours, preferably overnight.

❧ Bake, covered, at 350° F for 1 hour, or until meat is tender, basting frequently. Ribs may be refrigerated and reheated later. When ready to eat, simply drain off excess fat and place ribs on grill, 4 to 6 inches above medium-hot coals. Baste with reserved marinade or barbecue sauce. Cook, turning frequently, until crispy and richly glazed, about 15 to 20 minutes. The marinade is good served over rice.

Cheyennne River Ribs

Betty Pellatz
Cheyenne River Ranch, Douglas, Wyoming

Betty makes these barbecued ribs the first night out on cattle drives. She says they're easy to serve after camp is set up.

SERVES 6

3 lbs	pork or beef ribs
1	large onion, chopped
½ cup	water
¼ cup	vinegar
¼ tsp	black pepper
2 tbsp	brown sugar
1 tbsp	Worcestershire sauce
1 tbsp	dry mustard
1 tsp	salt
1 tsp	paprika

❧ Arrange ribs in a single layer in a large shallow casserole dish. Bake in a 350° F oven for 1 hour. Skim off fat.

❧ Combine remaining ingredients in a saucepan and simmer for 30 minutes. Pour over ribs and cook for 1 to 1 ½ hours, or until meat is tender.

Beans on the Trail

While there is no doubt that beans were a frequent menu item for cowboys on the trail, even the most avid fan of this versatile vegetable could eventually tire of them. One trail-hardened cowboy made his way to the restaurant in town and once there studied the menu at length. The cowboy couldn't read, however, and finally called the waiter to his table.

"You got any beans on this menu?" he asked.

The waiter pointed, "That is our only bean dish, sir."

"Are you absolutely sure that's all the beans on this menu?" the cowboy persisted.

"I'm sorry, sir," replied the waiter, "but that one dish is all we have in the way of beans."

"Fine," said the cowboy with an affable smile, "I'll have everything else but that."

Aunt Grace's Baked Beans

Bob Shultz
Prairie Canyon Ranch, Franktown, Colorado

Even trail-weary cowboys would have enjoyed this bean recipe. Growing up in South Dakota in the 1930s, Bob visited his Aunt Grace and Uncle John Way every chance he got. His Aunt Grace's baked beans were "the best." Fifty years later, Aunt Grace gave Bob the recipe by heart. Aunt Grace, who still lives in South Dakota, was 104 years old in December of 1996!

SERVES 6

2 cups	navy beans
	salt
2 tbsp	molasses
2 tbsp	ketchup
½ cup	brown sugar
1 tbsp	vinegar
¼ cup	onion, chopped
1 cup	bacon, diced
5	slices bacon
½ cup	tomato juice or sauce

❧ Cover beans with cold water and soak overnight. In the morning, drain and cover with clean water and a little salt. Bring to a boil and continue to boil for 20 minutes. Drain and put in a casserole dish.

❧ Add molasses, ketchup, brown sugar, vinegar, onion and bacon. Stir together well, then add enough water to just cover the mixture. Place strips of bacon over top and bake in 300° F oven. Pour tomato juice over beans part way through cooking. Take care not to let beans dry out while baking. Add a little hot water to keep beans moist. Bake for 3 to 4 hours.

Bob notes that if he forgets to soak raw beans, he uses 2 cans of pork and beans instead.

Bob sent along a few of his favorite sayin's. A couple of note are "Riding a jiggin' horse is like pounding your thumb with a hammer . . . it feels so good when you quit" and "There are two ways of arguin' with a woman . . . neither one works."

Barbecued Baked Beans

Michelle Schulte
Rock'n Bar Ranch, Big Cabin, Oklahoma

Serve this hearty dish with a green salad and sourdough biscuits.

SERVES 6 TO 8

4	14 oz cans pork and beans
1	onion, minced
1	green pepper, chopped
1 tbsp	mustard
1 to 2 tbsp	Worcestershire sauce
¼ cup	brown sugar
1 cup	barbecue sauce (hickory or smoke flavor)

ᕽ Combine all ingredients and cook for about 1 hour at 350°
F, or until thickened.

Calico Beans

Julie Saddler
Prairie Wind Ranch, Colby, Kansas

Bean dishes are a great time-saver on busy days. An array of bean choices makes this dish flavorable and attractive.

SERVES 8

2 lbs	ground beef
1	medium onion, chopped
1	14 oz can pork and beans
1	14 oz can kidney beans
1	14 oz can Great Northern beans
½ cup	bacon, cooked crisp, crumbled
1	14 oz can lima beans
½ cup	brown sugar
½ cup	ketchup
	salt and pepper to taste

❧ Brown ground beef and onion. Add remaining ingredients. Cook in a crockpot or Dutch oven for 4 hours, or however long chores take! Great served with cornbread.

Branding Beans

Kevin Heinle
Rock Hill Longhorns, McClusky, North Dakota

Try these beans with calf fries at branding time.

SERVES 25 TO 30

2 lbs	ground beef
1	large onion, chopped
1 lb	bacon, cooked crisp, crumbled
4	14 oz cans pork and beans
2	14 oz cans kidney beans, undrained
2	14 oz cans butter beans, drained
2	14 oz cans lima beans, drained
½ tsp	garlic powder
2 cups	ketchup
1 ½ cups	brown sugar
6 tbsp	white vinegar
2 tsp	liquid smoke
	salt and pepper to taste

❧ Brown ground beef with onions. Cook bacon well, drain and crumble. Add remaining ingredients and bake 1 to 1 ½ hours in 350° F oven. If a crockpot is used, cook 5 to 6 hours on low.

Buckhorn Exchange Bean Soup

George E. Carlberg C.E.C.
The Buckhorn Exchange Restaurant, Denver, Colorado

This soup has been on the menu at the Buckhorn Exchange for years. It's so popular they wouldn't dare take it off.

SERVES 6

1 lb	Great Northern beans
½ cup	onion, diced
3 oz	ham, diced
1 oz	chicken base
1 tsp	liquid smoke
1 tsp	garlic, minced
1 tsp	white pepper
½ gal	water
1 oz	cornstarch
½ cup	water

➢ Place all ingredients except cornstarch and water in a large casserole dish. Cover and cook in a 200° F oven for 8 hours. When beans are tender, remove from oven, place on stovetop and bring to boil. Add cornstarch and water to thicken and let simmer for 15 minutes.

The Chuckwagon

As moving cattle north to expanding markets and open ranges became big business, a few technological developments were inevitable. Perhaps the most important concerned the commissary department. Traveling over an unpopulated trail for several months with hired hands to feed necessitated having a vehicle designed to carry large amounts of provisions.

Charles Goodnight, surely one of the most resourceful cowboys who ever rode the range, saw the need for something better than the two-wheeled oxcart that had been in use. Goodnight's wagon and all that followed were four-wheeled conveyances with a bed or box, sideboards and metal bows over which a wagon sheet could be stretched to offer protection from the elements. At the back was the chuck box, a kind of kitchen cupboard on wheels with drawers and shelves to hold foodstuffs, pots, pans and eating utensils. The lowered door of the chuck box served as the cook's food preparation area.

The heavier supplies, such as flour, coffee, beans and meat, were carried in the wagon box along with the cowboys' bed rolls. On either side of the wagon were the water barrel and toolbox. Under the wagon was a box for the heavier cooking utensils, notably the Dutch oven as well as a rawhide cradle that housed the all-important fuel, usually wood or cowchips, that would be in short supply on the timberless plains.

The chuckwagon was an efficient and versatile piece of engineering with not an inch of wasted space. It seems a shame that it virtually disappeared with the demise of the trail drives and open range. There are still a few ranches that employ the chuckwagon for fall roundups and brandings, and each year the Calgary Stampede salutes the Old West with its exciting and world famous chuckwagon races.

Wrangler Soup

Gail Lander
Kedesh Ranch, Shell, Wyoming

Gail's soup is a big favorite with the wranglers after they come in from working outside in cold weather. It's a fast, easy recipe!

SERVES 15 TO 20

4 lbs	ground beef
2	onions, peeled, chopped
4	28 oz cans tomatoes
4	16 oz cans tomato sauce
4	14 oz cans whole kernel corn, drained
4	16 oz cans kidney beans
4	packages taco seasoning
	sour cream, chopped chives, sharp Cheddar cheese for garnish

❧ Brown beef in a large Dutch oven over medium heat. Add onion, tomatoes, tomato sauce, corn, kidney beans and taco seasoning mix. Simmer until flavors are blended. Garnish with sour cream, chives and cheese. Serve with tortilla chips.

Taco Soup

Mike and Glenda Wiles
Wiles Hamilton Nighthawk Ranch, Hamilton, Montana

This is a thick, hearty soup that freezes well.

SERVES 8 TO 10

2 lbs	ground longhorn beef
1	small onion, diced
1	14 oz can pinto beans, drained
1	14 oz can lima beans, drained
1	14 oz can red kidney beans, drained
1	16 oz can yellow hominy, drained
3	14 oz cans stewed tomatoes
1	8 oz can green chiles, drained
1	package dry ranch dressing
1 tsp ea	salt and pepper
1	package taco seasoning mix
½ cup	Cheddar cheese, grated
	tortilla chips or flour tortillas

~ Brown beef and onion in a large soup pot. Add remaining ingredients and simmer for 30 minutes or more. Top with grated cheese and serve with tortilla chips or warmed flour tortillas.

~ To vary the degree of hotness adjust the amount of green chiles. Rather than using canned beans, try a variety of dried beans and simmer in a crockpot.

Menudo

Kathy Burrows
Three B's of Colorado, Greeley, Colorado

This Mexican soup is traditionally served on the eve of Christmas or New Year's. Mexican men out on the town stop at all-night cafes for a Menudo nightcap. A bowlful is said to be good preventative medicine for hangovers.

SERVES 8 TO 10

8 lbs	tripe, honeycomb, ½-inch strips
1	package pork neckbones
8	cloves garlic, minced
2 tsp	dried coriander
6 quarts	water
1	package pork hocks
5	large onions, coarsely chopped
2 tbsp	salt
2 tbsp	Mexican red chili powder

❧ Pressure cook the above ingredients on low (5 pounds pressure) for 1 ½ hours, or cook slowly on top of stove for 2 to 3 hours.

The next morning add the following:

½ cup	Mexican red chili powder
1 tsp	dried cilantro
1	24 oz can white hominy

| 2 tsp | cumin |
| 2 tbsp | dried oregano |

❧ Heat the soup and serve with condiment dishes of chopped white onion, red pepper flakes and Mexican oregano. Have warm tortillas ready, individually rolled; flour tortillas are best.

Chicken Green Chili

George E. Carlberg C.E.C.
Buckhorn Exchange Restaurant, Denver, Colorado

Chicken is an interesting alternative to beef in this 1995 first-place winner of the Colorado Restaurant Association.

SERVES 4 TO 6

3 lbs	chicken thigh meat, ½-inch cubes
2	28 oz cans green chile strips
1	28 oz can tomatoes
10 oz	butter
⅓ cup	fresh garlic, minced
1 tbsp	jalapenos, diced
½ cup	flour
1 tbsp	salt
1 tsp	white pepper
3 tbsp	Worcestershire
1 tsp	sugar
1 tbsp	lime juice
⅓ cup	cilantro leaves, chopped

❧ Cover chicken with cold water and place over medium heat to cook. Drain, reserving stock.

❧ Place the green chile strips in colander to drain. Retain the liquid. Place the tomatoes in a colander to drain. Retain the liquid. Break the tomatoes into chunks.

❧ Melt butter in a heavy saucepan over high heat until

browned. Add the green chile strips, garlic and jalapenos and cook until the chiles have broken down and most of the moisture has evaporated.

❧ Add tomatoes to the chiles and continue to cook, until most of the moisture has evaporated. Add flour to the chiles and tomatoes, blend well, reduce heat and cook for 5 to 10 minutes.

❧ Add the retained juices, the chicken and stock. Stir well, working the roux from the bottom and side of the pan. Allow to come to boil, then reduce heat to a simmer.

❧ Add remaining ingredients. Add water as needed for desired consistency. Simmer for 10 to 15 minutes.

Tamale Pie

Mike and Glenda Wiles
Wiles Hamilton Nighthawk Ranch, Hamilton, Montana

An easy meal-in-a-dish, this recipe can be made with longhorn or any lean ground beef.

SERVES 4 TO 6

2 lbs	ground longhorn beef
1	package taco seasoning
2	14 oz cans kernel corn, drained
2	14 oz cans stewed tomatoes
3 tbsp	salsa
½ cup	Cheddar or Jack cheese, grated

🖎 Brown beef, then add remaining ingredients. Simmer. Pour into a casserole dish and cover with cornbread topping (recipe page 105). Bake at 400° F for 20 to 25 minutes. Remove from oven and sprinkle with cheese.

Chicken à la King

Jeannine Lahrman
Tarryall River Ranch, Lake George, Colorado

This is a great way to use leftover chicken or turkey.

SERVES 4 TO 6

4	10 oz cans cream of mushroom soup
3	soup cans of milk
6 cups	cooked chicken, chopped
2 tbsp	dry sherry
¼ cup	butter
2 cups	peas and carrots
1 cup	mushrooms, sliced
2 tbsp	flour
¼ tsp	paprika

❧ Pour soup and milk into a saucepan and simmer. Sauté chicken with sherry and butter until tender, then put in pan with the soup mixture. Cook for 1 hour. Add remaining ingredients and continue cooking for 15 to 20 minute. Serve over white rice or in a bread bowl.

Rainbow Trout, Cajun-Style

Montana is famous the world over for its trout fishing. Each year thousands of anglers converge on the state to try their hand at catching a few. This recipe is similar to the "blackened fish" made popular by Cajun cooks and is a delicious way to serve freshly caught trout.

SERVES 4

1 ½ tsp	paprika
¾ tsp	pepper
½ tsp ea	salt, oregano, chili powder and dry mustard
¼ tsp	dried thyme
⅛ tsp	cayenne pepper
4 oz	trout fillets
2 tsp	olive oil
2 tsp	fresh parsley, chopped
1	green onion, chopped
	lemon wedges

❧ Combine spices and herbs and set aside. Pat fillets dry and place on broiler rack. Lightly brush both sides of fillets with oil and sprinkle with spice-herb mixture.

❧ Place the broiler rack 4 to 6 inches from the heat and broil for 4 to 5 minutes, until the fish flakes easily with a fork. Place on a serving dish and sprinkle with fresh parsley and green onion. Serve with lemon wedges.

Barbecued Trout

Idaho's lakes, rivers and streams offer an abundance of rainbow, cutthroat and Dolly Varden trout. This recipe is an easy and appetizing way to prepare the catch of the day.

SERVES 4

3 to 4 lb	trout, filleted, skin on
2 tbsp	teriyaki or soy sauce
1 tbsp	lemon juice
1 tsp	horseradish
2 tbsp	brown sugar
2 tbsp	jalapeno juice
2 tbsp	barbecue sauce
1 tbsp	seasoned salt

ã Place fish fillets in a shallow casserole dish. In a separate bowl, combine remaining ingredients for the marinade. Pour over fish fillets. Turn fish to coat both sides. Cover and let sit for 1 hour, turning every 15 minutes.

ã Barbecue, skin side down, over hot coals, until fish flakes easily. Brush occasionally with marinade while cooking.

Salmon Steaks à l'Orange

This recipe is a quick and elegant dish. Serve with new potatoes and fresh asparagus.

SERVES 4

4	salmon steaks, 1-inch thick
	salt and freshly ground pepper
⅓ cup	orange juice
⅓ cup	white wine
	grated zest of 1 orange
2 tbsp	orange liqueur (optional)

❧ Coat a nonstick frying pan with olive oil and place over medium-high heat. Generously salt the salmon steaks and cover with freshly ground pepper.

❧ Place steaks in pan and cook on one side until golden brown. Turn and continue cooking on other side.

❧ Pour remaining ingredients over salmon and continue cooking until fish is cooked through and flakes easily with a fork. If serving asparagus, place in frying pan with salmon steaks, pour orange sauce over top, cover and cook until salmon and asparagus are tender. Add more orange juice as necessary.

❧ Serve immediately with orange sauce drizzled over salmon and asparagus.

[Snacks & Desserts]

Peanut Butter Cookies

Gail Lander
Kedesh Ranch, Shell, Wyoming

According to Gail, these cookies disappear so fast, you'll wonder if you even made them. The folks at Kedesh Ranch eat so much peanut butter that they buy it in 5 pound containers. Often!

MAKES 3 TO 4 DOZEN COOKIES

1 cup	peanut butter
1 cup	soft shortening
1 cup	granulated sugar
1 cup	brown sugar, firmly packed
2	eggs
2 ½ cups	flour
1 tsp	baking powder
1 ½ tsp	baking soda

&● Mix peanut butter, shortening, sugars and eggs. Blend dry ingredients in a separate bowl, then stir into wet mixture. Chill. Heat oven to 375° F. Form dough into balls the size of large walnuts. Roll in sugar. Place 3 inches apart on lightly greased cookie sheet. Flatten with a fork to form a crisscross pattern. Bake 10 to 12 minutes.

Cowboy Cookies

Julie Saddler
Prairie Wind Ranch, Colby, Kansas

Opening gates is not a desired task, but Julie comments that when she bakes these cookies, everyone is so anxious to get back to the ranch to sample a few it seems she doesn't have to open as many gates!

MAKES 4 DOZEN COOKIES

1 cup	white sugar
1 cup	brown sugar
1 cup	shortening
2	eggs
2 tsp	vanilla
2 cups	flour
½ tsp	salt
1 tsp	baking soda
½ tsp	baking powder
1	16 oz package chocolate chips
2 cups	quick oats
1 cup	walnuts, chopped

❧ Cream both sugars and shortening. Add eggs and vanilla and mix well. In a separate bowl, combine dry ingredients, then add to sugar mixture. Mix well. Add chocolate chips, oatmeal and nuts. Drop by the spoonful on lightly greased cookie sheet. Bake at 350° F for 10 minutes. Try not to overbake as these cookies are best if a little softer.

Oklahoma Crude Cake

Carol Toole
Mangum, Oklahoma

This cake is to be enjoyed when not counting calories.

SERVES 12 TO 16

Cake

1 cup	butter
4 tbsp	cocoa
2 cups	sugar
1 tbsp	vanilla
4	eggs
1 ½ cups	flour
1 cup	coconut
1 ½ cups	pecans, chopped
1	9 oz jar marshmallow cream

Icing

½ cup	butter
6 tbsp	milk
3 ½ tbsp	cocoa
1 to 1 ½	boxes of powdered sugar

❧ To prepare cake, melt butter. Add cocoa, sugar, vanilla and eggs. Combine flour, coconut and pecans in a separate bowl and add to butter mixture. Beat 2 minutes and pour into a 9 x 13-inch pan. Bake at 350° F for 35 to 40 minutes. Remove from oven. Spread with marshmallow cream while cake is still hot. Cool before icing.

🍃 To prepare icing, combine butter, milk and cocoa. Heat until butter is melted. Remove from heat, add sugar and beat well. Spread on cooled cake. Do this carefully, making sure marshmallow cream does not show through.

Homestead Cake

Jean Kary
Reverse K Box Ranch, Norris, South Dakota

Jean first baked this cake when she cooked for ranch hands back in the 1950s. Called Homestead Cake in the 1900s, the cake came to be known as Depression Days Cake in the 1930s and World War II Cake in the 1940s. The fact that it's eggless, butterless and requires no milk makes it as popular today as it was in earlier times.

SERVES 12 TO 16

2 cups	water
2 cups	brown sugar
2 tsp	shortening
½ to ⅔ cups	raisins
1 tsp	salt
1 tsp	ground cinnamon
1 tsp	ground cloves
3 cups	flour
1 tsp	baking soda
2 tsp	hot water

Combine water, sugar, shortening, raisins, salt, cinnamon and cloves in a saucepan. Boil 5 minutes, then set aside until cool. Dissolve baking soda with water and add. Mix well. Turned into a greased cake pan. Bake 1 hour at 350° F. This cake is just as tasty plain as it is with the addition of a few nuts, dates or dried fruit.

Applesauce Layer Cake

Jay and Lynn Contway
Great Falls, Montana

One of the Northwest's great cowboy artists, Jay has successfully told the story of cowboy life and times in his bronzes, which are prized by collectors all over North America.

During Jay's bachelor days, he liked to stop at his sister Cathy's to scrounge a meal or snack. Cathy could always be counted on to have something on the stove. One lunchtime, however, she was called away so she turned the stove off and left. When she returned all that remained of her meal was a dirty plate and empty pots and pans. She has threatened to lock Jay out of her house ever since!

Lynn, who ran the Prince of Wales Tea Room when she lived in Alberta, says this recipe comes from the Contway family where it's been popular since the 1950s.

SERVES 10 TO 12

1 cup	seedless raisins, washed and dried
2 ½ cups	pastry flour
— or —	
2 ¼ cups	all-purpose flour
3 tsp	baking powder
½ tsp	salt
1 tsp	ground cinnamon
1 tsp	ground nutmeg
½ tsp	ground ginger
10 tbsp	butter
1 cup	sugar
2	eggs, well beaten

⅓ cup   cold coffee

1 cup   thick applesauce, sieved

➔ Grease two 8-inch round layer cake pans and line bottoms with greased paper.

➔ Sift flour, baking powder, salt, cinnamon, nutmeg and ginger together. Mix in raisins. In a separate bowl, cream butter and gradually blend in sugar. Add eggs a little at a time, beating well after each addition. Add flour mixture to creamed mixture about a quarter at a time, alternating with cold coffee and applesauce. Combine lightly after each addition. Turn into prepared pans.

➔ Bake in a preheated 350° F oven for 25 to 30 minutes. At serving time, put layers together with additional applesauce between. Top with whipped cream and sprinkle with nutmeg.

Irish Cream Cake

Jeannine Lahrman
Tarryall River Ranch, Lake George, Colorado

SERVES 10 TO 12

Cake

1	package yellow cake mix without pudding
1	small package instant vanilla pudding mix
4	eggs
½ cup	shortening
1 cup	Irish cream liqueur
¾ cup	walnuts or pecans, finely chopped

Glaze

½ cup	butter
¼ cup	water
1 cup	white sugar
½ cup	Irish cream

❧ To prepare cake, combine all ingredients and beat for 4 minutes on high. Grease and flour a Bundt or angel food pan. Sprinkle nuts in bottom of pan, add mixture and bake for 45 to 55 minutes at 350° F. Cool slightly, then glaze.

❧ To prepare glaze, melt butter in a saucepan. Stir in water and sugar. Boil for 5 minutes, stirring constantly. Remove from heat and stir in Irish cream. Prick top of cake and spoon glaze evenly over top.

Grand Marnier Cake

Bake this cake for the next birthday celebration or ranch picnic.

SERVES 10 TO 12

Cake

¾ cup	butter
2 cups	white sugar
2	eggs
1 tsp	vanilla
2 ½ cups	flour
2 tsp	baking soda
½ tsp	salt
2 cups	buttermilk or soured milk

Sauce

¼ cup	slivered fresh orange peel
1 cup	sugar
1 cup	water
1 cup	orange juice concentrate
3 tbsp	Grand Marnier liqueur

The night before, slice the outer peel from an orange, being careful not to include any of the white. Cut the peel into thin slivers. Soak the peel in the sugar and water overnight. This takes the bitter flavor out of the peel.

ಖ To prepare cake, cream butter and sugar. Add eggs and vanilla and beat well. In a separate bowl, combine flour, baking soda and salt. Add creamed mixture alternately with buttermilk. Mix until just blended after each addition.

❧ Pour cake batter into a greased 10-inch Bundt pan. Bake at 350° F for 40 minutes, or until done. Remove cake from oven and cool 10 minutes before attempting to turn out onto a serving tray. It's essential to allow this cake to cool or it will come out of the pan in chunks!

❧ To make sauce, combine orange peel and liquid with remaining ingredients. Place in a saucepan and simmer for 5 minutes. Pour half the syrup over the warm cake. Serve with remaining sauce spooned over cake slices. Top with whipped cream and slices of fresh orange.

Wild Bill Hickok

Like most cowboys, Wild Bill Hickok enjoyed nothing better than pie. And it seems the sometimes lawman was particularly fond of apple pie. One afternoon Wild Bill was enjoying a wedge of his favorite sweet in a hotel restaurant in Ellsworth, Kansas, then a busy railhead for incoming Texas cattle. Hickok, a man not long on ceremony, had the pie firmly in his right hand.

Enter Bill Thompson, someone with whom Hickok had a long-standing feud. Thompson, seeing his adversary with his right hand occupied with the pie thought there would be no better opportunity to draw down on Hickok than at that moment. And he did. One can only assume that Thompson didn't know that Wild Bill was just as adept at drawing and shooting with his left hand as he was with his right. He was soon to find out.

Thompson's gun never left its holster. As the unfortunate challenger went crashing down, taking tables, plates and coffee cups with him, Hickok went on with the business of eating his pie. (That's the way witnesses to the event told it, and everybody knows a cowboy wouldn't fib about a thing like that.)

Apple Crumb Pie

Make this pie when apples are in abundance during the fall. There's nothing better than the smell of fresh apple pie on a crisp fall day.

SERVES 6

¾ cup	flour
½	brown sugar
¼ cup	butter
4 to 5	apples
½ cup	white sugar
1 ½ tsp	ground cinnamon
1 tsp	lemon juice
1	unbaked single-crust pie shell

❧ Blend flour, brown sugar and butter and set aside. Wash, core and slice apples. Layer apples in pie shell and sprinkle with white sugar, cinnamon and lemon juice. Spread brown sugar mixture evenly over top and bake in 375° F oven for 45 minutes, or until apples are soft.

Grandma's Peanut Butter Pie

Julie Saddler
Prairie Wind Ranch, Colby, Kansas

Since its invention in 1890, peanut butter has become popular throughout the country and is a definite staple of ranch life. Julie's husband likes this pie with chocolate syrup drizzled over top.

SERVES 6

¾ cup	sugar
	pinch of salt
3 tbsp	cornstarch
2 cups	milk
3	egg yolks
3 tbsp	peanut butter
2 tbsp	butter
1 tsp	vanilla
1	single-crust pie shell, baked and cooled

ᐧᐧ Mix together sugar, salt, cornstarch and milk and cook over medium heat until thick, stirring constantly. Beat egg yolks. Add a spoonful of hot mixture to egg yolks and stir. Add egg yolks and cook for 4 minutes. Remove from heat and add peanut butter, butter and vanilla. Pour into pie shell and chill.

Strawberry Meringue Pie

Virginia Purdy
Purdy Ranch, Buffalo, Wyoming

In Wyoming, springtime brings the strawberry harvest and brand-ing season to the Purdy Ranch. One of the ranch's city guests makes the finest dessert ever! He gets invited back every year as he also tends the branding irons.

SERVES 6

Filling

3 oz	cream cheese
2	egg yolks
1	10 oz can sweetened condensed milk
¼ cup	lemon juice
2 to 3 cups	strawberries, sliced (raspberries may be substituted)
1	single-crust pie shell, baked and cooled

Meringue

4	egg whites
½ cup	sugar
¼ tsp	salt
	pinch of cream of tartar

❧ To prepare filling, soften cream cheese, then mix with a fork until smooth. Beat egg yolks and mix with cream cheese. Add milk, lemon juice and fruit. Pour into pie shell.

❧ To make meringue, place egg whites, sugar, salt and cream

of tartar in a large stainless steel bowl and place over a pan of simmering water. Whisk until mixture is lukewarm. Remove from heat and beat until egg whites form stiff peaks. Cover pie with meringue and brown in oven.

Huckleberry Pie

There's no more satisfying way to end a meal than with a slice of fresh fruit pie.

SERVES 6

3 cups	huckleberries
	(blueberries may be substituted)
3 tbsp	flour
3 tbsp	butter
¼ cup	corn syrup
3 tbsp	lemon or orange juice
⅓ cup	brown sugar
2 tsp	vanilla
1	unbaked double-crust pie shell

❧ Mix berries with flour. Place in a pie plate that has been lined with pastry. Dot with bits of butter. Mix syrup, juice, brown sugar and vanilla. Pour over berries. Cover with a solid or lattice crust. Bake 10 minutes at 400° F. Lower heat to 325° F and bake another 15 minutes, or until done.

Huckleberry Buckle

SERVES 6

Cake

½ cup	butter, room temperature
½ cup	sugar
1	egg
1 cup	flour
1 ½ tsp	baking powder
¼ tsp	salt
½ cup	low fat milk
2 cups	huckleberries (blueberries may be substituted)

Topping

¼ cup	butter
1 cup	sugar
½ cup	flour
½ tsp	ground cinnamon
	whipped cream

❧ Cream butter with sugar. Add egg and beat 1 minute. In a separate bowl, combine flour, baking powder and salt. Add to butter mixture alternately with milk. Pour into greased 9-inch square pan, spreading evenly. Cover with berries.

❧ To prepare topping, cream butter and sugar, add flour and cinnamon and blend until crumbly. Sprinkle over berries.

❧ Bake at 375° F for about 45 minutes, or until golden brown. Serve with whipped cream, if desired.

[Preserves]

Blueberry-Rhubarb Preserves

Julie Saddler
Prairie Wind Ranch, Colby, Kansas

This jam is a real treat on freshly baked biscuits.

MAKES 4 TO 5 CUPS

5 cups	rhubarb, diced
1 cup	water
4 cups	sugar
1	16 oz can blueberry pie filling
2	packages raspberry Jell-O

❧ Mix rhubarb, water and sugar in pot and cook 8 to 10 minutes. Add pie filling and Jell-O. Cook until Jell-O is dissolved. Pour into sterilized containers. Refrigerate or freeze.

Skillet Jams

Kathy Burrows
Three B's of Colorado, Greeley, Colorado

Here's a quick way to make jam out of odds and ends from the refrigerator. If you follow the recipes carefully, the jams will set nicely and keep in the refrigerator for a couple of weeks.

Once the jam is cooked, pour into two halfpint jars with tight-fitting lids. Cover and refrigerate until set, about 6 hours. Each recipe makes about 2 cups.

Blueberry

1 pint	blueberries, mashed
2 tbsp	powdered fruit pectin
½ tsp	butter
1 cup	sugar

☙ In a 12-inch skillet, heat blueberries, pectin and butter over medium-high heat, stirring constantly until mixture boils. Stir in sugar and heat to boiling. Boil 1 minute and remove from heat.

Raspberry

Prepare as above but use

3 cups	raspberries
1 ½ cups	sugar
1 tbsp plus 1 tsp	powdered fruit pectin

🍃 Press half the raspberries through the sieve to remove some of the seeds before mixing with other ingredients.

Peach

Prepare as above but use

1 lb	peaches, peeled, pitted, and mashed
2 tbsp	powdered fruit pectin
2 tsp	fresh lemon juice
1 cup	sugar

🍃 To peel peaches dip in boiling water for about 20 seconds. Remove with a slotted spoon and rinse under cold water. Peel and pit peaches, then mash.

[Beverages]

Sock Coffee

It was fine for trail-driving cowboys to look forward to and receive lots of good hot coffee after a day of herding reluctant longhorns. But what about those who traveled alone, people like line riders, outlaws and loners. Most had no coffee pot but still liked their coffee. It was for people like these that sock coffee was invented.

1	sock (clean if possible)
1	pot
	coffee
	water

Spoon medium ground coffee into sock, making sure to add one extra spoonful for the sock. Tie sock and immerse in a pot of boiling water. Cook until desired strength is achieved or until the color of the sock matches the color of the ones you're wearing!

The Beverage of Choice

Contrary to long-held opinions fostered by pulp westerns and movies, it was coffee, not whiskey, that was the beverage of choice for the early cowboys. Crossing an icy, swollen river, taking a long, cold shift of night herd duty or spending several hours in the saddle during a prairie thunderstorm—all were guaranteed to bring cowboys into camp at a high lope looking for coffee. And every camp cook knew that the coffee had to be three things: hot, strong and plentiful. A chuckwagon might run short of flour, beans or salt pork without incident, but if the coffee ran out, the drive could come to a complete standstill. All this for a drink that, until the Civil War, was consumed almost solely by the wealthy.

It was Arbuckle's that was the brew of choice—"Arbuckle's, the coffee that won the West"—the later ads quite rightly proclaimed. Its popularity may have had as much to do with the container as the coffee itself. Arbuckle's was shipped in wooden crates, and on the prairie where lumber was at a premium, Arbuckle's crates served as chairs, cupboards and shelving for chuckwagons, ranch houses and blacksmith shops.

The Arbuckle's marketing team was pretty sharp, too. In each bag of coffee was a piece of peppermint candy. The candy became the reward for the cowboy who volunteered to do the grinding for the cook. The candy was so popular among sweet-toothed cowboys that the issue of who was going to grind the coffee was sometimes settled by a more or less friendly fight.

Cowboys on night duty who weren't particularly musical could often be heard softly reciting the words from Arbuckle's labels to the herd. Arbuckle's became more than a drink to be consumed with every meal and a whole lot of times in between. It became a vital part of the history of the West.

Campfire Coffee

If you lean toward more conventional beverage preparation (or if you're out of socks), this is the way camp cooks have made coffee for more than a century.

MAKES 12 TO 14 CUPS

1	large enamel coffee pot
3 to 4 quarts	water
2 to 3 heaping tbsp	coffee
	whiskey (optional depending on time of day)

❧ Heat water in pot over coals. Add coffee to boiling water and simmer. Remove from heat when done and add a dash of cold water to settle the grounds.

Brandy Slush

This slush is made from ingredients that are easy to keep on hand and is a refreshing summer party beverage.

SERVES 12

9 cups	water
2 cups	brandy
1	12 oz can frozen lemonade concentrate
1	12 oz can frozen orange juice concentrate
	mint leaves for garnish

ᨃ Mix all ingredients together in a large container that can be stored in the freezer. Freeze overnight, or until slushy. To serve, scoop into glasses and garnish with mint leaves.

The Canadian West

Alberta, British Columbia, Saskatchewan

WE RECENTLY ASKED A PRAIRIE OLD-TIMER HOW HE would describe Western Canadian cuisine. He stroked his chin for a while and finally said, "You know, I'm not sure as we've got us one o' them cuisines, but if we have, it'd probably lean towards meat 'n' potatoes." The old gentleman, with his typically unassuming Canadian response, was probably right. As often as not, the farms and ranches of the Canadian West serve up, in countless combinations and often ingenious ways, variations on the old fella's description. In a land where climate can take a terrible physical toll and where the landscape itself presents one of the challenges to overcome, the connection between hearty and hardy is natural.

With seeding, harvesting, haying, calving and branding taking up a good part of the calendar year and with the focus on fast and nutritious, one of the variations cooks often turn to is that practical favorite: the casserole. There isn't much that any self-respecting cook can't put in a casserole dish, stick in the oven and turn into something that our old-timer would approve of. But it would be an oversimplification to suggest that there is no distinctly Western Canadian cooking. As in other parts of North America, the cuisine is influenced by the people who settled the land. French Canadians, Scandinavians, British, Irish, Scottish and Ukranians, for example, have all influenced what is set on rural Western Canadian tables at meal time. And the land itself has put its stamp on the region's cuisine as well. There is nothing more Canadian than maple syrup, saskatoon berry pie, Canadian goose and freshly baked bread made with the world's finest wheat. And we'd be remiss if we didn't mention one other group of people who have influenced the food Canadians eat. Historically, the first building you saw when driving into a Canadian prairie town was the grain elevator, but the second building was likely the Chinese café, most often a family-run business that had been around almost as long as the town itself. When Canadian ranchers tired of their meat and potatoes, they were likely to pack the family into the pickup and head for the nearest café for a meal of chow mein, chop suey and chicken fried rice.

[Starters]

Deviled Eggs

Roy Warhurst
Sons of the Pioneers

Deviled eggs were a popular addition to Canadian hors d'oeuvres trays in the 1920s and continue to be popular today. Thanks to Roy Warhurst of the legendary cowboy music group the Sons of the Pioneers for contributing this tasty appetizer.

SERVES 8

8	hard-boiled eggs
½ tsp	salt
½ cup	mayonnaise
¼ cup	green pepper, finely chopped (optional)
1 tsp	dry mustard
¼ tsp	pepper
1 cup	flakes of ham or chicken
¼ cup	celery, finely chopped

❧ Cook eggs, then peel and cut in half lengthwise. Scoop out yolks, mash and combine with remaining ingredients. Return to whites and sprinkle with paprika. Because there will be extra filling, Roy suggests serving the remaining filling on crackers.

Pita Pocket Surprise

Amy Kohlruss
Lloydminster, Saskatchewan

Western Canada's newer immigrants have put their stamp on the cuisine of the region. Here is a Greek-inspired appetizer that would nicely complement an hor d'oeuvres tray of feta cheese and black olives. Sprinkle a little oregano and drizzle a bit of olive oil over the cheese and olives and, along with these pita pockets, you've got great before-dinner munchies.

SERVES 18 TO 24

24	small pita pockets, cut in half
1	package 7-vegetable soup mix
2 cups	sour cream
1 cup	mayonnaise
1	package frozen spinach, thawed, drained, chopped

❧ Combine all ingredients except pita pockets. Blend well. Spoon a teaspoon of filling onto each pita pocket half. Place on serving tray. Cover and chill overnight.

Mexican Antipasto

Connie Jackson
SJ Hereford Ranch, Gadsby, Alberta

*Today, dishes in the Canadian West feature a cross-cultural infl-
uence. Here is a antipasto with a Southwest twist!*

SERVES 10 TO 12

6	slices bacon, cooked crisp, crumbled
1	8 oz package cream cheese
½ cup	sour cream
	dash garlic salt
1	large avocado, mashed
¼ tsp	lemon juice
1	tomato, finely chopped
1	4 oz can green chiles
4	green onions, chopped
¼ cup	ripe olives, sliced
¼ cup	green olives, sliced
1	8 oz bottle taco sauce, hot, thick and chunky
1 cup	Cheddar cheese, finely grated

ва Cook bacon well, crumble and set aside. Combine cream
cheese, sour cream and garlic salt and layer in the bottom of a
9-inch pie plate. Combine avocado, lemon juice, tomato and
chiles and layer over cream cheese. Sprinkle with bacon, green
onion and olives. Spread taco sauce over top and sprinkle with
grated cheese. Serve with taco chips.

Pan-Fried Scampi

Amy Kohlruss
Lloydminster, Saskatchewan

This Italian-inspired appetizer is a special treat for holiday get-togethers.

SERVES 8 TO 10

2 to 3 lbs	jumbo shrimp
	butter
2 to 3	cloves garlic
	flour
	salt and pepper to taste
	fresh lemon juice

❧ Peel and devein shrimp. Melt butter in a frying pan and sauté garlic. Roll shrimp in flour and fry in garlic butter. Turn shrimp once during frying. Once shrimp curl up, they're done. Remove from pan, season with salt and pepper and squeeze lemon juice over. Serve warm.

Wrangler's Chicken Wings

Tara Giles
Giles Ranching, High River, Alberta

Tara serves these wings often for ranch get-togethers or picnics. They work well as an appetizer or as a main meal with rice and a fresh garden salad.

SERVES 4

3 lbs	chicken wings
1	egg, beaten
1 cup	flour
1 cup	oil
3 tbsp	soy sauce
3 tbsp	water
1 cup	brown sugar
½ tsp	salt

❧ Cut wings in half. Dip in beaten egg and then in flour. Fry in oil until golden brown. Remove to a shallow casserole dish.

❧ Mix soy sauce, water, sugar and salt and pour over wings. Bake at 350° F for 30 minutes, spooning sauce over wings several times until they are thoroughly glazed. Serve hot or cold.

Prairie Oysters

Mary Lou Grabowsky
Douglas Lake Ranch, Douglas Lake, British Columbia

Established in 1884, Douglas Lake Ranch covers thousands of acres in British Columbia's interior plateau cattle country. Much of the Douglas Lake Ranch land is carefully managed to provide grazing for the cattle. The traditional image of the Western cowboy lives on at this Canadian ranch with cattle drives, brandings and campfire cooking still part of the ongoing routine. Prairie oysters are a special treat at annual brandings.

SERVES 12 TO 14

	oysters from last branding
1 cup	milk
½ cup	fine breadcrumbs
½ cup	poultry seasoning
½ tsp	garlic powder
	salt and pepper to taste
½ cup	butter
	green relish
	sour cream
	chives, chopped

❧ Double skin prairie oysters. Soak in milk. Combine breadcrumbs, poultry seasoning, garlic, salt and pepper. Roll oysters in crumb mixture. Fry in butter until golden. Serve hot with green relish or sour cream and chives.

Butterflied Prairie Oysters

Rusty Lucas
Lucasia Ranch, Claresholm, Alberta

The youngest contributor to the cookbook, Rusty is also a good hand at a branding or team roping. And he's the main man when it comes to calf fries in the foothills west of Claresholm!

SERVES 10 TO 12, DEPENDING ON HOW HUNGRY THE CREW IS!

	raw prairie oysters, cleaned and butterflied
½ cup	milk
2	eggs, beaten
1	package soda crackers, finely crushed
	butter for frying

➤ Dip each butterflied prairie oyster in milk, then in egg and finally, in crushed crackers. Fry in melted butter until golden brown.

[Breads]

Grandma Lil's Biscuits

Helen Gilchrist
Cypress Cattle Co., Maple Creek, Saskatchewan

This recipe is similar to the baking powder biscuit recipe that was taught in home economics classes during the 1920s. Helen is the third generation in her family using the recipe. She says cowboys always love them.

MAKES 24 TO 30 BISCUITS

5 cups	flour
5 tsp	baking powder
1 tsp	salt
½ cup	sugar
½ cup	butter
3 cups	milk

🍂 Mix all ingredients except milk until mixture is fine and mealy. Add milk to make a soft dough. Roll out ½-inch thick and cut into rounds. Sprinkle with sugar. Raisins may be added to soft dough. Bake at 400° F for about 12 minutes, or until golden brown.

Chuckwagon Biscuits

Lauren Hitchner
Hitchner Quarter Horses, Longview, Alberta

Lauren's mother, who was born in eastern Colorado in 1902, swears this recipe was popular on the wagon trains and with many chuck-wagon cooks. The biscuits are tender and moist when fresh, yet durable enough to travel in saddle bags.

MAKES 2 DOZEN BISCUITS

1	package active dry yeast
2 ½ tbsp	warm water
3 ¼ cups	unsifted all-purpose flour
2 ¼ tsp	baking powder
⅛ tsp	baking soda
1 tbsp	sugar
½ tsp	salt
½ cup	shortening
1 cup	buttermilk
	melted butter

❧ Dissolve yeast in warm water and set aside. Sift flour, baking powder, baking soda, sugar and salt. Cut in shortening. Add buttermilk to yeast mixture. Combine yeast and flour mixtures, kneading slightly.

❧ Roll out to ½-inch thickness and cut with a 2 ¼-inch biscuit cutter. Place on a greased baking sheet and brush lightly with melted butter. Let rise 30 minutes. Bake in 350° degree oven for 25 to 30 minutes.

Renie's Ranch Biscuits

Renie Blades
Rocking P Ranch, Nanton, Alberta

*Biscuits such as these surely came north with the first cattle herd.
The West was won on beans and biscuits!*

MAKES 18 BISCUITS

1 cup	flour
4 tsp	baking powder
1 tsp	cream of tartar
½ tsp	salt
2 tsp	sugar
½ cup	shortening
¾ cup	milk
— or —	
½ cup	milk
and	
¼ cup	mayonnaise

❧ Sift dry ingredients, cut in shortening until crumbly, then
add liquid. Knead gently a few times. Lightly flour surface and
roll out dough to about ⅔-inches thick. Cut with cookie cutter, drinking glass or empty tin cup. Bake for 10 to 15 minutes
at 400° F, or until lightly browned.

Cream Scones

Scones came to the Canadian West via Scottish immigrants. These scones are great for breakfast or afternoon tea. Strawberries and whipped cream make a nice addition.

MAKES 12 TO 18 SCONES

2 cups	flour
4 tsp	baking powder
½ cup	butter
½ cup	sugar
2	eggs, beaten
½ cup	cream

❧ Sift flour and baking powder together. Blend butter into mixture. Add sugar, eggs and cream. Roll out dough on a floured surface and cut into squares or circles. Bake in 400° F oven for 20 minutes, or until lightly browned.

Allana's Two-Hour Buns

Allana Annett and April Beckley
Three Bars Cattle and Guest Ranch, Cranbrook,
British Columbia

Three Bars Ranch guests enjoy fresh buns along with the Western fare that is served in the big log dining room.

MAKES 5 DOZEN BUNS

4 tbsp	quick-acting yeast
16 cups	flour, more or less
6 cups	very warm water
1 cup	sugar
⅔ cup	oil
3 tsp	salt
4	eggs, lightly beaten

🌢 In a large bowl, mix together yeast and half the flour. Add remaining ingredients and stir. Keep adding flour until dough is soft but not sticky. Turn out onto a floured surface and knead slightly.

🌢 In a large bowl, add 1 to 2 tablespoons oil. Place dough in bowl and turn so dough is coated with oil. Cover with plastic and a damp cloth, then place in a warm area for 15 to 30 minutes, or until dough has doubled in size.

🌢 Punch down and form into balls approximately 2 inches in diameter. Place on greased baking sheets and let rise for 45 to 60 minutes. Bake at 350° F for 15 minutes.

Two-Hour Dinner Buns & Cinnamon Buns

John and Kathy Duffy
Doubletree Ranch, Buck Lake, Alberta

Kathy's husband, John, is a saddle bronc rider, stock contractor and one of Canada's finest western artists, particularly noted for his rodeo drawings and paintings.

These delicious buns will surely win first place at any fair. Freeze them in packages of 6 and take out a new package every day in order to have the freshest buns possible. The cinnamon buns never get to the freezer as they usually disappear the first day.

MAKES 2 DOZEN DINNER BUNS AND 2 DOZEN CINNAMON BUNS

4 tbsp	quick rising yeast
8 cups	flour
2	eggs, beaten
8 tbsp	white sugar
½ cup	butter, melted
3 cups	lukewarm water
1 tbsp	salt

❧ Mix yeast with 4 cups of flour. In a separate bowl, add eggs, sugar, butter and water. Make sure the mixture is warm; if not, reheat to lukewarm. Add the flour-yeast mixture and beat until smooth.

❧ Add salt to 3 cups of flour and stir into dough. Turn out

onto a floured surface and knead in enough flour to make a slightly sticky dough. You may need more or less flour depending on the size of eggs and how much water was used.

🐾 Cover and let rise in a warm place for 15 minutes. Punch down and let rise another 15 minutes. Punch down again and divide dough in half. Form half the dough into dinner buns and place on a greased baking sheet. Let rise 1 hour, then bake at 350° F until golden brown, approximately 15 minutes.

🐾 Divide the remaining dough into two equal parts. Roll out two ¼-inch thick rectangles. Spread each piece of dough with approximately ½ cup of softened butter, then cover with a thick layer of brown sugar, sprinkle generously with cinnamon. Sprinkle one or both pieces with raisins, if desired.

🐾 Roll the dough lengthwise and cut each roll into 12 equal slices. Grease two 9 x 12-inch cake pans with butter and sprinkle a thin layer of brown sugar on the bottom. Place cinnamon rolls in pans. Cover and let rise in a warm place for 1 hour. Bake at 350° F for 15 minutes, or until golden brown. Using metal pans will make softer buns.

Merry's White Bread

Jack and Merry Vandervalk
Vandervalk Ranch, Claresholm, Alberta

Don't let the ingredients fool you. This recipe makes a nice loaf or buns. Adding Sunnyboy cereal gives the bread a grainy texture.

MAKES 5 OR 6 LOAVES

1	potato
4 tbsp	shortening
½ cup	molasses or honey
2 cups	oatmeal porridge
1 cup	Sunnyboy cereal (optional)
1 tbsp	salt
4 cups	water
2 tbsp	yeast
12 cups	flour, more or less

❧ Cook potato. Mash, then add shortening and molasses or honey. Combine porridge, Sunnyboy cereal (if using) and salt with water and add to potatoes. Add yeast and flour. Mix well to form a spongy dough. Let rise. Punch down and form into loaves or buns. Let rise again and bake in 350° F oven.

Rancher's Whole Wheat Bread

Jack and Merry Vandervalk
Vandervalk Ranch, Claresholm, Alberta

This bread recipe is a favorite in the Vandervalk house anytime, but it tends to be used most during branding season. Merry also makes it up as buns, which are tasty with sliced roast beef.

MAKES 9 OR 10 LOAVES

1 large tbsp	honey
18 cups	whole wheat flour
7 ½ cups	hot water
1 ½ cups	whey powder
4 tbsp	liquid lecithin
½ tsp	vitamin C powder
3 tbsp	fast-rising yeast
2 tsp	salt

❧ Add honey and about 6 cups flour to water. Then add whey powder, lecithin, vitamin C powder and yeast and mix. Add salt and enough flour to clean the bowl, about 18 cups total. Beat in large bread mixer for 10 minutes, or knead thoroughly by hand. Let rise once. Punch down. Let rise a second time. Form buns or put in greased loaf pans. Let rise again and bake at 375° F for 20 minutes for buns or 30 minutes for bread.

Yorkshire Pudding

Kim Hitchner
Longview, Alberta

For many Canadians of British descent, Sunday dinner consisted of roast beef, yorkshire pudding, mashed potatoes and gravy. Yorkshire pudding is traditionally baked in the same pan as the roast, but a quick, easy way to prepare the pudding is in muffin tins.

SERVES 6

4	eggs
¼ tsp	salt
1 cup	milk
1 cup	flour
6 tbsp	solid shortening

❧ Beat eggs with salt. Add milk and flour and beat well. Put 1 tablespoon of shortening in each of 6 large muffin tins. Heat muffin tins in 475° F oven until shortening melts, then pour in pudding mixture. Bake at 475° F until puddings start to rise, then reduce heat to 450° F and continue baking until done, about 15 minutes. Serve with roast beef gravy poured generously over the top.

Potato Dumplings

Evelyn Livingstone
Val Terra Herefords, Vermilion, Alberta

Dumplings were known as doughboys when they first became popular in the 1930s. These dumplings are a unique and delicious accompaniment to stew.

SERVES 6 TO 8

2 cups	potatoes, cooked, riced
2 tbsp	shortening, melted
1	egg, slightly beaten
½ tsp	salt
	pepper to taste
⅛ tsp	ground nutmeg or parsley

❧ Combine all ingredients and mix thoroughly. Divide into 12 balls. Chill. Drop into gently boiling stew and cook for about 12 minutes in covered pot.

Creamed Corn and Bacon Muffins

Sherri-Dale Henry
Henry Cattle Co., High River, Alberta

Sherri served these at one of her family's cookbook recipe-tasting dinners and they were a big hit. Absolutely a keeper, these muffins.

MAKES 12 MUFFINS

1 cup	yellow cornmeal
½ cup	milk
1 cup	flour
4 tsp	baking powder
½ tsp	salt
1	egg
1 ½ cup	creamed corn
½ cup	shortening, melted
½ lb	bacon, cooked crisp, crumbled

Combine cornmeal and milk in a bowl and set aside. In a separate bowl, combine dry ingredients and set aside. Mix egg with creamed corn, then combine all ingredients together. Spoon batter into greased muffin tins and bake at 400° F for 20 minutes.

Quick Cheddar Bread

Kim Hitchner
Longview, Alberta

Try this recipe when you're looking for a fast way to put fresh bread on the table.

SERVES 8 TO 10

3 ⅓ cups	biscuit mix
2 cups	Cheddar cheese, grated
1 ¼ cups	milk
2	eggs, lightly beaten
½ tsp	dill weed

᪶ Combine biscuit mix and cheese together. Add milk and eggs. Pour into greased and floured loaf pan. Bake at 350° F for approximately 45 minutes, or until toothpick inserted in center comes out clean.

Orange Butter Buns

Hugh and Billie McLennan
The McLennan Ranch, Kamloops, British Columbia

Billie's husband, Hugh, is host of the popular syndicated radio program Spirit of the West, *a celebration of cowboy culture.*

Billie says this recipe is a family favorite and is served every Christmas morning. It's become such a favorite, in fact, that if someone in the McLennan family can't get home for Christmas, Billie makes a batch and sends it to them. The recipe is known around the McLennan household as "Mom's Christmas Buns." Billie found the recipe in one of her old family cookbooks many years ago.

MAKES 24 BUNS

1 tbsp	yeast
¼ cup	warm water
1 cup	sugar
1 tsp	salt
2	eggs
½ cup	sour cream
¾ cup	butter, melted
2 ¾ to 3 cups	flour
1 cup	coconut
2 tbsp	grated orange rind
¾ cup	sugar
½ cup	sour cream
2 tbsp	frozen orange juice concentrate
¼ cup	butter

❧ Soften yeast in warm water. Stir in ¼ cup sugar, salt, eggs, sour cream and 6 tbsp butter. Gradually add flour to form a stiff dough, beating after each addition. Cover. Let rise in a warm place until light and doubled in bulk, about two hours.

❧ Combine remaining sugar, ¾ cup coconut and orange rind and set aside. Knead dough on a floured surface about 15 times. Divide dough in half and roll into two 12-inch circles. Brush each circle with melted butter. Sprinkle with sugar-coconut mixture and cut into wedges. Roll, starting at wide end and roll to point. Place rolls, point-side down, in a greased 9 x 13-inch baking pan. Cover, let rise in a warm place until doubled, about 1 hour. Bake at 350° for 25 to 30 minutes, until golden brown.

❧ Make glaze by combining remaining ingredients in a saucepan and boil 3 minutes, stirring occasionally. Pour glaze over hot buns. Sprinkle top with remaining coconut. These freeze very well, so may be made well before the busy season.

Saskatoon Muffins

Don and Joyce Ulrich
Ulrich Polled Herefords, Medicine Hat, Alberta

Picking wild, ripe saskatoons is a favorite summer activity in Alberta and Saskatchewan. These muffins make a great snack with a cup of steaming hot tea.

MAKES 12 LARGE MUFFINS

½ cup	melted butter
1	egg lightly beaten
1 cup	milk
½ cup	sugar
1 ¾ cups	flour
3 tsp	baking powder
½ tsp	salt
1 cup	fresh or frozen saskatoons
1 tsp	lemon peel

❧ Mix butter, egg and milk. Add sugar and mix well. Add dry ingredients, stirring only until combined. Fold in berries and add lemon peel. Bake in greased muffin tins at 375° F for 20 minutes.

Top of the World Apple Pancakes

Michele Sadler
Top of the World Guest Ranch,
Fort Steele, British Columbia

Michele's grandma used to make these pancakes for breakfast during the fall season. Michele now uses the recipe for Sunday morning breakfasts at the ranch.

SERVES 2

1 ½ cups	flour
1 cup	milk
¼ tsp	salt
1 to 2 cups	sliced green apples
½ heaping tsp	cinnamon
¼ cup	sugar

≈ Mix flour, milk and salt. Add sliced apples. Heat vegetable oil in a cast iron frying pan to a fairly high temperature. Spoon batter into frying pan. While pancakes are cooking, combine cinnamon and sugar. When pancakes are finished, remove from pan, spread with butter and top with cinnamon-sugar mixture. These pancakes will melt in your mouth!

[Salads & Side Dishes]

Broccoli Salad

Barbara Hughes
Chinook Ranch, Longview, Alberta

Barbara makes this salad for branding days, Christmas dinner, community potlucks and picnics.

SERVES 8 TO 10

1 tbsp	white vinegar
3 tbsp	sugar
½ cup	mayonnaise
5 cups	broccoli, broken into small florets
¼ cup	red onion, chopped
½ lb	bacon, cooked crisp, crumbled
1 cup	sunflower seeds, unsalted
1 cup	raisins
1	stalk celery

ᵛ Combine vinegar, sugar and mayonnaise and set aside. In a separate bowl, combine remaining ingredients and add mayonnaise mixture. Marinate for about 5 hours. This salad keeps well in the refrigerator so may be made well in advance.

Top of the World Ranch Salad

Michele Sadler
Top of the World Guest Ranch,
Fort Steele, British Columbia

The Sadlers enjoy this salad at outdoor picnics and Saturday night cookouts.

SERVES 10 TO 12

2	heads romaine lettuce, shredded
1	head iceberg lettuce, shredded
3	large fresh tomatoes, chopped
2	14 oz cans red kidney beans, drained
2 cups	Cheddar cheese, grated
1	bag tortilla chips, crushed (taco or ranch flavored)
1	8 oz bottle Ranch salad dressing

In a large salad bowl, shred lettuce, add tomatoes, kidney beans and cheese and mix. Add chips and dressing just before serving.

Happy Trails Salad

Diane Davis
Okotoks, Alberta

Diane is the wife of well-known equine veterinarian Dr. Gordon Davis. If you are in the horse business in Alberta, I guarantee that you know who Gord is. Gord attends as many brandings as his schedule permits and enjoys riding the mountain pastures and punching cows on summer weekends.

SERVES 4 TO 6

8 cups	romaine lettuce, shredded
½ cup	feta cheese, crumbled
1 cup	seedless grapes, red and green
¼ cup	red onion, thinly sliced
¼ cup	olive oil
2 tbsp	lemon juice
1 tsp	sugar
	pepper to taste

In a large salad bowl, shred lettuce, then add cheese, grapes and onion. Mix oil, lemon juice, sugar and pepper and toss with salad just before serving.

Canned Vegetable Salad

Ann Britton
Flying Lazy B, Rokeby, Saskatchewan

This is a handy salad to prepare for unexpected guests.

SERVES 12 TO 14

2 lbs	green beans
2 lbs	yellow beans
2 lbs	carrots
4	medium onions
5 lbs	cucumbers
2 lbs	celery
2 lbs	corn kernels, frozen or canned

🍂 Cut vegetables into medium-size pieces. Mix together and pack solidly into hot sterilized jars. To each quart add

1 scant tsp	celery seed
1 scant tsp	mustard seed
1 tsp	salt
⅓ cup	white sugar
⅓ cup	vinegar

🍂 Fill jars with boiling water and seal tightly. Boil for one hour in canner. To serve, drain off juice and mix vegetables with your choice of salad dressing or mayonnaise.

Pasta Salad

Peggy Herman
Herman's Horned Herefords, Bindloss, Alberta

Peggy's mother made this for brandings or wiener roasts on Sundays.

SERVES 6 TO 8

4 cups	rotini pasta, cooked
2 or 3 cups	raw vegetables, chopped
¼ cup	vinegar
½ to ¾ cup	vegetable oil
1	package pasta dressing mix

❧ Choose a variety of vegetables such as celery, green onions, cucumbers, carrots, radishes, red peppers, broccoli and tomatoes. Combine vegetables and pasta in a large salad bowl. Mix vinegar and vegetable oil with pasta dressing mix. Prima works best for the dressing mix. Add dressing to salad and mix well. Chill at least 1 hour, or overnight. Stir occasionally.

Red Cabbage

Ann Britton
Flying Lazy B, Rokeby, Saskatchewan

This is an early pioneer dish that is especially good with roast beef or pork.

SERVES 6 TO 8

½ to ¾ lb	bacon, cooked crisp, crumbled
¼ cup	sugar
½ cup	onion, chopped
1	medium red cabbage, grated
1	tart apple, grated
2 tbsp	vinegar
10 to 12	whole cloves

❧ Fry the bacon until crisp. Set aside. Add sugar to the bacon fat in pan and cook for two minutes on medium heat. Add onion and fry for five minutes. Add cabbage, apple, vinegar and cloves. Reduce heat to low and cook for 45 to 60 minutes, stirring occasionally. Add up to ½ cup water to keep moist. Sprinkle with bacon before serving. This is best if made a day ahead. Just reheat to serve.

Scalloped Cabbage

Evelyn Livingstone
Val Terra Herefords, Vermilion, Alberta

Try this old-fashioned creamy vegetable dish with mashed potatoes and roast pork.

SERVES 4 TO 6

3 cups	cabbage, grated
2 tbsp	flour
½ tsp ea	salt and pepper
1 cup	milk
½ cup	buttered breadcrumbs
	cheese, grated for garnish

In a casserole dish, layer cabbage, then sprinkle with flour, salt and pepper. Pour milk over cabbage and top with bread-crumbs. Bake at 350° F for 30 minutes. Add grated cheese for extra zip.

Bierocks

Leona Wurst
Calgary, Alberta

Leona says this dish is an old German recipe and a favorite with family members. This dish freezes well. Just reheat for a fast snack!

MAKES 3 TO 4 DOZEN

1	large head cabbage, finely chopped
2	medium onions, finely chopped
¼ to ⅓ lb	lard
	salt and pepper to taste
1 recipe	white bread dough

❧ Melt lard in a large frying pan. Add finely chopped cabbage and onions. Season with salt and pepper. Stir occasionally. Set aside.

❧ Roll out bread dough fairly thin. Cut dough into squares. Spoon 1 to 2 tablespoons cabbage mixture onto each square (do one square at a time). Bring up ends of dough around the cabbage and pinch together. Turn each square upside down and place on greased baking sheet. When all squares are done, set covered baking sheets in a warm place for 45 minutes to rise. Bake in 350° F oven for 30 minutes, or until nicely browned.

Bacon Peas

Hugh and Billie McLennan
The McLennan Ranch,
Kamloops, British Columbia

This is an old family recipe that originated with Hugh's maternal grandparents who were of Russian and German descent. Over the years it has been modified to fit into our modern world of frozen vegetables and canned soup. Here it is as Billie makes it today.

SERVES 8 TO 10

1	package bacon, diced
1	large onion, chopped
2	10 oz cans consommé
2 tbsp	flour
1	large package frozen peas

❧ Cook bacon and onion in a large frying pan. Drain bacon fat and add consommé. Heat to boiling and thicken with flour mixed with a small amount of water. This can be made ahead of time.

❧ Shortly before serving, put peas in a small amount of salted water and bring to a boil. Drain and add to consommé sauce. Serve. Cut recipe in half for smaller crowds.

Fiddler's Green Bean Casserole

Jane Hawley Sutherland
High River, Alberta

Jane is a fiddle player and says that this recipe was given to her by another fiddler from Louisiana, Kentucky. When Jane dropped off her recipes, she stuck them in the door of one of the editor's houses and a chinook wind came up and blew them into the hills. The next time she brought them, it cost that editor $20 to buy raffle tickets for the Bullrider's Benevolent Fund!

SERVES 4 FIDDLERS FINE

2	14 oz cans French-style green beans, drained
1	10 oz can cream of mushroom soup
1	large onion, diced
1	14 oz can dried onion rings

  Mix green beans, soup and onion in a small casserole dish. Sprinkle dried onion rings on top. Cover pan tightly and cook at 375° F for 20 minutes. Remove cover and lightly brown top for about 5 minutes.

Lima Bean Casserole

Lauren Hitchner
Hitchner Quarter Horses, Longview, Alberta

This may be one of the world's few edible lima bean dishes! Try this recipe even if you think you don't like lima beans; you'll change your mind after one taste of this delicious casserole. It's dynamite served with ham, pork or anything barbecued.

SERVES 6 TO 8

1 lb	dried lima beans
½ cup	butter
1 tbsp	molasses
¾ cup	brown sugar
1 tbsp	dried mustard
1 tbsp	salt
1 cup	cream
6	slices bacon

❧ Soak lima beans overnight. Cook in boiling water until almost tender. Drain and set aside. To make sauce, heat butter over low heat in a small saucepan. Add remaining ingredients except bacon, stirring until sugar is dissolved and sauce is smooth.

❧ Place lima beans in a casserole dish, add sauce and top with slices of bacon. Bake at 350° F for 1 hour.

Barley Casserole

V.E. Hanson
Calgary, Alberta

This is a flavorable accompaniment to baked chicken or fish.

1	medium onion, chopped
1 tbsp	butter
1 cup	barley
1	10 oz can mushrooms, drained
— or —	
1 cup	fresh mushrooms, sliced
2	10 oz cans beef or chicken consommé

 Sauté onion in butter. Combine all ingredients in a casserole dish and bake at 350° F until liquid is absorbed.

California Ranch Rice

Donna Graves
Peavine Ranch, Williams Lake, British Columbia

Donna is the wife of professional horse trainer Art Graves and mother of pro rodeo cowboys Wade and Lee.

SERVES 8 TO 10

1 cup	onions, chopped
2	cloves garlic, minced
4 tbsp	butter
4 cups	cooked rice
2 cups	sour cream
1 cup	small curd cottage cheese
1	bay leaf, crushed
— or —	
1 tsp	oregano
	salt and pepper to taste
14 oz	whole green chiles, cut into strips
— or —	
4 to 5	fresh jalapenos, chopped
2 ½ cups	Cheddar cheese, grated

In a large frying pan, sauté onions and garlic in butter until limp. Add rice, sour cream, cottage cheese, bay leaf, salt and pepper and mix together. In a greased casserole dish, put a layer of rice mixture, a layer of chiles and a layer of cheese, reserving ½ cup of cheese. Repeat layers ending with rice. Bake at 375° F for 25 minutes. Sprinkle reserved cheese over the top and return to oven for 20 minutes.

Top of the World Cheese-Potato Casserole

Michele Sadler
Top of the World Guest Ranch,
Fort Steele, British Columbia

A recipe used for family reunions for years, this dish is another favorite at the ranch's Saturday night cookouts.

SERVES 6

1	10 oz can cream of chicken or mushroom soup
1 cup	sour cream
1 cup	Cheddar cheese, grated
1 bag	hash brown potatoes
½ cup	butter, melted
2 tbsp	butter, melted
2 cups	crushed corn flakes

In a large bowl, combine soup, sour cream, cheese, potatoes and ½ cup butter. Pour into a greased casserole dish. Top with mixture of remaining melted butter and crushed corn flakes. Bake at 350° F for 45 minutes.

Simple Perogy Casserole

Rayel Robinson
Sundre, Alberta

Two-time Canadian Barrel Racing champion and National Finals Rodeo qualifier Rayel Robinson claims she doesn't really cook, but from all accounts that's not the case.

This is an excellent, speedy dish to prepare for unexpected company. Perogies are a Ukrainian dish, common throughout Alberta and Saskatchewan.

SERVES 8

2	packages frozen perogies
1	package bacon, cooked crisp, crumbled
1	medium onion, chopped
⅛ cup	butter
1 quart	cream

❧ Boil perogies until they float to top of water. In a frying pan, sauté onions in butter. Combine all ingredients in a casserole dish and bake at 350° F for 30 minutes. Serve hot.

[Main Dishes]

English Brown Stew

Jeanette Alwood Rousseau
The Bar U Ranch, Pekisko, Alberta

Jeanette was raised on the historic Bar U Ranch where her father Stu Alwood was the ranch foreman. This stew was a favorite with the Alwood family during the 1940s.

SERVES 4

2 lbs	stewing beef
	flour, salt and pepper
	oil
1	clove garlic
½ tsp	paprika
½ tsp	ground allspice
1 tsp	sugar
1 tbsp	lemon juice
1 tsp	Worcestershire
2 cups	tomato juice
2	onions
5	potatoes, medium
4	carrots
¾ cup	celery, diced

🥄 Dredge stewing beef in flour, salt and pepper. Brown in oil. Add remaining ingredients and simmer on low heat for 1 to 2 hours.

Kate's Chili

John and Kathy Duffy
Doubletree Ranch, Buck Lake, Alberta

Kathy developed this recipe over the years by trial and error, adding different ingredients according mood. This is the mild "company" version. Serve with biscuits and grated cheese.

SERVES 6

2 lbs	ground beef
1	large onion, chopped
1	clove garlic, minced
2	green peppers, chopped
1	red pepper, chopped
1	28 oz can red kidney beans
1	28 oz can brown beans
1	10 oz can mushrooms, sliced
1	19 oz can tomatoes, diced
2 cups	whole kernel corn
3 tbsp	chili powder
1 tsp	parsley flakes
¼ tsp	jalapeno flakes
¼ tsp	cayenne pepper
1 tsp	salt
1 tbsp	Tex-Mex complete seasoning mix

 Brown meat in a large frying pan, add onions and garlic. Continue cooking until onions are transparent. Add spices and transfer meat mixture to a large pot. Put the remaining ingredients in the frying pan and heat through. Add to meat and cook.

Red-Eye Stew

Ruth Pickett
Pickett Ranching Ltd., Bassano, Alberta

This recipe can be doubled for a large crowd. To save time, make the stew ahead and heat just before serving.

SERVES 12

½ cup	flour
3 tsp	salt
½ tsp	pepper
3 lbs	stewing beef
½ cup	oil
4 lbs	onions, thinly sliced
2	cloves garlic
1	12 oz can beer (optional)
3 tbsp	soy sauce
2 tbsp	Worcestershire sauce
2 tbsp	steak sauce
1 tsp	thyme
2	bay leaves
4 cups	tomato juice
8	potatoes, peeled, diced
8	carrots, diced
2 cups	frozen peas

  Combine flour, salt and pepper. Dredge meat in flour mixture and brown in hot oil. Add onions and garlic and cook until onion is transparent.

ᘓ Add beer, soy sauce, Worcestershire and steak sauce. Add thyme and bay leaves and bring to a boil. Lower heat and simmer for 1 hour. Add tomato juice and simmer 30 minutes. Add potatoes and carrots and cook until vegetables are tender. Add peas and heat through. Remove bay leaves before serving.

Cowboy Stew

The Ranchman's Restaurant
Calgary, Alberta

The Ranchman's was named Country Club of the Year for 1995 and 1996.

SERVES 10

1 oz	vegetable oil
2 lbs	stewing beef
½ cup	flour
1	large onion, chopped
½	bunch celery, chopped
½ lb	carrots, diced
1 ½ lbs	potatoes, diced
1	6 oz can tomato paste
¼ bottle	HP sauce
¼ oz	liquid gravy color
2 oz	beef bouillon powder
¼ tbsp	sweet basil
¼ tbsp	oregano
½ tsp	cayenne pepper
1 tbsp	black pepper
1 tbsp	salt

❧ Heat oil in a large heavy-bottomed pot. Dredge beef pieces in flour and brown in oil. Add remaining ingredients and simmer on low heat for 1 to 1 ½ hours, or until vegetables are tender. If stew is too thick, add a small amount of tomato juice or water.

Spiced Kettle of Beef and Vegetables

Renie Blades
Rocking P Ranch, Nanton, Alberta

SERVES 8 TO 10

2 lbs	stew meat
1 tsp	salt
½ tsp ea	pepper and paprika
1	onion, chopped
6 cups	water to cover meat
1 to 2 tsp	pickling spice, secured in cheesecloth
2 cups	carrots, chopped
1 cup	celery, chopped
3 cups	potatoes, chopped
1	turnip, chopped
1 cup	green peas
1	14 oz can tomatoes (optional)
	salt and pepper to taste

❧ Combine meat, salt, pepper, paprika, onion, pickling spice and water and simmer for 3 hours. The secret to good stew is cooking it long and slow.

❧ When meat is tender, add the remaining ingredients and continue cooking until vegetables are tender. Thicken the stew before serving with ¼ cup flour or cornstarch blended with ½ cup cold water. Add salt and pepper.

Cowboy Music

The music we call cowboy music didn't happen by accident. It originated on the trail drives in the second half of the last century and was as important to the success of the drive as good grass and plentiful water. Nights were especially problematic during the drives north. The spooky longhorns seemed to look for any excuse to stampede, and the scream of a nearby cougar, a clap of thunder or an accidental gunshot were more than enough to set them to running.

To counter as much as possible the likelihood of a stampede and the often disastrous consequences, the trail drivers took turns doing herd duty at night, talking and more often singing to the cattle. There were songs that were standards, known to all the riders, and there were compositions that were created right there in the saddle. And for the cowboy who couldn't or wouldn't sing, there were labels that could be recited (Arbuckle's coffee bags were a favorite).

The music endured and a century later cowboy songs are enjoying a resurgence in popularity that parallels the increased interest in the whole cowboy mystique. Hollywood's singing cowboys, Roy and Gene, may have hung up their guitars, but a new generation of artists is keeping the tradition alive, none better than the Sons of the Pioneers and Canada's Ian Tyson.

Onion Soup

Ian and Twylla Tyson
Ian Tyson Cutting Horses, Longview, Alberta

Ian's latest CD is entitled All the Good 'Uns. *It is the newest contribution to what has become one man's social history of the West set to music.*

SERVES 4

5 cups	onions, thinly sliced
2	cloves garlic, crushed
6 tbsp	butter
1 to 2 tsp	salt
½ tsp	dry mustard
	dash thyme and white pepper
3 cans	chicken broth
1 tbsp	tamari
3 tbsp	dry white wine
1 tsp	honey, optional
	Monterey jack or Swiss cheese, grated
	croutons

৵ Place onions and garlic in soup pot with butter. Lightly salt. Cook slowly, being careful not to brown too much. Add mustard, thyme and pepper and mix well. Add remaining ingredients. Cook slowly, covered, for at least 30 minutes. Serve topped with croutons and cheese.

Hamburger Soup

Don and Joyce Ulrich
Ulrich Polled Herefords, Medicine Hat, Alberta

*This recipe is handy for those days when you have extra workers for
lunch, but nobody has time to cook. Served with fresh buns, cold cuts
and cheese, it becomes a full meal.*

SERVES 4 TO 6

1 ½ lbs	ground beef
1	medium onion, chopped
	salt and pepper to taste
½ tsp	thyme
2 tsp	parsley
2	bay leaves
1 tsp	Worcestershire sauce
1 to 2 tsp	seasoning salt
1	10 oz can tomato soup
1	28 oz can tomatoes, chopped
2 cups	water
3 to 4	carrots, finely chopped
2	stalks celery, finely chopped
8 tbsp	barley

❧ Brown meat and onions in a large Dutch oven. Add
remaining ingredients and simmer at least 2 hours. Longer is
better.

The Best Bean Dish

"We were taking fifteen hundred head of Diamond bar cattle to the railhead in Abilene. It was a beautiful autumn day and we were three days from delivering the herd when we stopped for the night. I shook the dust from my trail-weary body and settled down to cook myself a pot of my famous Mexican Kidney Beans and Tomatoes. Under a now-threatening sky, Muji, our Hindu horse wrangler, had a similar purpose in mind and soon the glorious aroma of his legendary Vindaloo sauce drifted across the campsite. Suddenly, a lightning bolt struck the herd and a stampede of snorting, frightened beefsteak came crashing through camp, overturning everything before running wild out into the prairie night. Hours later, after gathering and calming the terrified bovines, Muji and I returned to our stewing concoctions to find that in the mayhem they had been mixed and blended into one pot. After a cautious tasting we both declared it to be the finest bean dish west of the Pecos!

"Okay, I confess, the story is pure bull and the recipe comes from my mom in San Francisco!"

–DAVID WILKIE

Rose's Curried Mexican Beans

David Wilkie
El Mando Rancho, Turner Valley, Alberta

One of the West's outstanding musicians and songwriters, David's recent release is the very successful Cowboy Celtic.

SERVES 4 TO 6

¾ tsp	dry mustard
1 tsp	curry powder
1 tbsp	hot water
6	slices bacon
1	medium onion, minced
½ cup	green pepper, chopped
1	28 oz can kidney beans, partially drained
1	28 oz can tomatoes, chopped
1	7 oz can deviled ham
3 tbsp	molasses
	salt to taste

✿ Blend dry mustard and curry powder with hot water. Dice 1 slice bacon with onion and green pepper and combine with mustard-curry mixture. Place in a large casserole dish with beans, tomatoes, ham, molasses and salt. Put remaining strips of bacon on top and bake in 400° F oven for 30 minutes, or until bacon is browned.

Jean's Beans, at Home or in Camp

Jean Hoare
Driftwillow Ranch, Stavely, Alberta

Jean doubts if her beans are ever the same twice. She starts with a mixture of dry beans, as many as seven different kinds, adds ham joints, pork hocks, salt pork or bacon ends, then the sauce.

SERVES 6 TO 8

1 ½ cups	assorted dried beans
	water to cover beans
1	large onion
8	whole cloves
¼ cup ea	molasses, brown sugar, maple syrup
½ cup	ketchup or chili sauce
1 tbsp	dry mustard
1 tsp	salt
1 tbsp	Worcestershire sauce
½ cup	boiling bean water
	diced salt pork, bacon ends or leftover baked ham

❧ Beans may include one or more of the following: small white navy beans, the larger Great Northern beans, pinto, limas, kidney, blackeye, garbanzos or chick peas.

❧ Put assorted beans into a large heavy pot and cover with water, about three to four times as much water as beans. Let stand overnight. Drain and cover with fresh water. Cover, bring to a boil, then simmer slowly until tender. Test for doneness of beans by blowing on them. If done, the skins will blow off. The small navy bean will take the longest to cook. Do not add meat and other ingredients yet or the beans will not soften. They should boil alone in water until tender.

❧ When beans are tender, drain, reserving the liquid. Stick whole cloves into the onion and add to the cooked beans. Add molasses, brown sugar, maple syrup, ketchup, dry mustard, salt, Worcestershire sauce and half the reserved liquid. Add meat. Cover and bake at 250° F for 6 to 9 hours, adding extra bean water or more ketchup if the mixture becomes dry. Uncover for the last half hour and adjust seasonings, if necessary.

❧ For camp, prepare the beans up to the final baking stage. Then dig a whole at least 4 inches deeper than the heavy iron bean pot. Prepare enough coals to have a good layer underneath the pot and on top of it. Put the bottom layer of hot coals into the hole, then lower the pot into the hole, covering the lid with foil to keep out any dirt. Cover with remaining coals and bury with at least 3 inches of dirt. Bake in the pit for at least 4 hours, watching that the dirt stays in place, thus holding in the heat.

❧ A final word about beans. To speed up the soaking process, cover the dried beans with water, bring to a boil and simmer for 2 minutes. Then remove from heat and let stand, tightly covered, for 1 hour. Blanching beans like this is equivalent to about 8 hours soaking.

Papa Roy's Baked Beans

Roy Warhurst
Sons of the Pioneers

This is a quick and easy way to prepare beans that have lots of old-fashioned Western flavor.

SERVES 8 SONS OF THE PIONEERS

5 to 6	slices Canadian bacon, diced
½	green pepper, chopped
1	medium onion, chopped
2	19 oz cans pork and beans
¼ cup	brown sugar
1 tbsp	prepared mustard
½ cup	ketchup

Sauté bacon until almost cooked. Then add green pepper and onion. Cook until onion is clear and bacon is nearly done. Add remaining ingredients and place in a casserole dish. Bake at 325° F for 1 hour.

Flying Lazy B Beans

Ann Britton
Flying Lazy B, Rokeby, Saskatchewan

This is a great recipe to take to a barbecue or pot luck supper.

SERVES 8 TO 10

4	14 oz cans of pork and beans
1	package onion soup mix
— or —	
1	large onion, diced
1 tbsp	dry mustard
1 cup	brown sugar
½ cup	vinegar
¾ cup	ketchup
2	cloves garlic, crushed

&. Mix all ingredients in a pot and simmer until heated through.

OH Beans

Eileen Walker
OH Ranch, Longview, Alberta

This recipe comes from Eileen's good friend Shirley Armstrong. It's a great dish for large gatherings.

SERVES 50

3	large onions, chopped
3	green peppers, chopped
2	red peppers, chopped
3 lbs	bacon, diced
2 gallons	pork and beans
6	14 oz cans lima beans, drained
6	14 oz cans green beans, drained
6	14 oz cans kidney beans, drained
6	14 oz cans mushrooms, drained
3 cups	brown sugar
6	small jars chili or barbecue sauce (about 48 ounces)

❧ Sauté onions, peppers and bacon. Combine all ingredients and place in large casserole dish. Cook in a 325° F oven for 1 ½ to 2 hours.

Beef Wellington

Jean Hoare
Driftwillow Ranch, Stavely, Alberta

SERVES 4

2 lbs	beef tenderloin
½ lb	mushrooms, finely chopped
3 tbsp	butter
1 tsp	flour
	salt and freshly ground pepper to taste
	prepared puff pastry

≥ The easiest way to prepare puff pastry is to buy it in the frozen food section of the supermarket.

≥ Remove any muscle tissue left on the tenderloin. Place in an uncovered roasting pan and roast no more than 20 minutes at 400° F. This precooking step is important, otherwise the meat might not be cooked enough.

≥ Chop mushrooms. Melt butter in a frying pan, add mushrooms, flour, salt and pepper. Stir for several minutes. Roll out the puff pastry and spread with the mushroom mixture. Place partially cooked tenderloin in the center of the pastry, roll pastry over meat and make a bottom seam. With extra puff pastry, make decorations to add to the top of the Wellington. Bake according to the instructions on the puff pastry package. Serve with tomatoes and mushrooms carved in interesting shapes.

Billie's Branding Roast

Hugh and Billie McLennan
The McLennan Ranch, Kamloops, British Columbia

Billie says this roast is a favorite with their ranch's branding crew because it comes out tender, moist and tasty. She likes it, too, because it is easy to prepare ahead of time, which allows Billie to look after her duties at the branding fire.

SERVES 30 TO 40

1	16 to 18 pound roast (whole outside bottom)
	Worcestershire sauce
	salt, pepper and garlic salt to taste

Leave about ¼-inch fat on one side of roast. Sprinkle roast generously on all sides with Worcestershire sauce and plenty of salt, pepper and garlic salt. Wrap in tinfoil and make an enclosure that closes at the top as there will be a fair amount of juice when cooked. Place tinfoil-wrapped roast in a pan in a 150° F oven and forget about it for 12 hours.

When the branding is done, the beef will be done. Go to the kitchen, wash your hands, and sit down to eat. Serve hot beef on buns and use the juice for dipping or gravy.

Texas-Steak Pot Roast

Ann Britton
Flying Lazy B, Rokeby, Saskatchewan

A taste of Texas up in Canada! The addition of lime juice and cumin gives this pot roast a tangy flavor.

SERVES 4

1	round steak
	pepper to taste
1 tbsp	olive oil
1 cup	beef stock
1 cup	salsa
2 tbsp	lime juice
2	onions, sliced
2	cloves garlic, chopped
2 tsp	cumin

❧ Liberally sprinkle meat with pepper and sear in oil on both sides. Remove meat and set aside. Stir beef stock into pan and bring to a boil, scraping off all brown bits. Stir in salsa, lime juice, onions, garlic and cumin. Place steak in a roaster and add stock. Bake at 325° F for 2 to 2 ½ hours.

Three Bars Ranch Ribs

Allana Annett and April Beckley
Three Bars Cattle and Guest Ranch,
Cranbrook, British Columbia

A succulent, tender meat dish that is excellent served with fresh bread.

SERVES 15 TO 20

25	racks beef back ribs
2 cups	chicken broth
1 cup	ketchup
1 tbsp	soy sauce
1 cup	liquid honey
1 cup	brown sugar
8 cups	vinegar

❧ Precook ribs in a 375° F oven for 30 minutes to cook off some of the fat. Drain. Cool and cut ribs into 3 pieces. Place in a large deep casserole dish. Combine remaining ingredients and pour over ribs. Cook in a 250° F oven for approximately 4 hours, or until tender. Baste ribs occasionally during cooking.

Joan's Oven-Barbecued Ribs

Joan Hager
Wainwright, Alberta

Canadian Finals Rodeo Barrel Racing qualifier Joan Hager not only handles horses well, she's also an excellent cook.

SERVES 4 TO 6

3 to 4 lbs	pork spareribs
2 tbsp	butter
1	small onion, chopped
¾ cup	ketchup
½ cup	brown sugar
¼ cup	vinegar
1	clove garlic, crushed
2 tsp	Worcestershire sauce
	salt and pepper to taste

ᨆ Place ribs in a roaster or baking dish. Combine remaining ingredients in a large saucepan and boil 4 to 5 minutes. Add to ribs. Cook at 350° F for 2 hours.

Mock Duck

Fay and Randy Dunham
Dunham Training Stables, Turner Valley, Alberta

This recipe was Fay's mother's favorite.

SERVES 4 TO 6

1	whole round steak
	salt and pepper to taste
2 cups	breadcrumbs
2 tbsp	onion, chopped
2 tbsp	celery, chopped
1 tsp	sage
1 tsp	salt
¼ tsp	pepper
1 cup	boiling water
¼ cup	butter, melted

❧ Have butcher cut one whole round steak. Season with salt and pepper. Make stuffing by combining breadcrumbs, onion, celery, sage, salt and pepper. Toss stuffing ingredients together and spread on steak. Roll up like a jelly roll and secure with butcher string. Brown on all sides in hot oil in a frying pan, then place in a roasting pan. Add boiling water and melted butter.

❧ Cover and bake for 1 hour at 300° F to 350° F. Extra water may be added halfway through cooking to keep the meat from drying out. Let sit 10 minutes, then slice and serve with gravy.

Rustler's Pork Tenderloin

Pat Haynes
Haynes Ranching, Longview, Alberta

This is one of Pat's gourmet recipes that she uses for a pleasant evening of entertaining.

SERVES 4

⅛ cup	butter
½ cup	celery, chopped
¼ cup	onion, chopped
4 cups	soft breadcrumbs
1 tsp	salt
½ tsp	pepper
1 tsp	sage or poultry seasoning
8	pork tenderloin
8	slices bacon

❧ Melt butter in a frying pan, add celery and onion and cook slowly. Remove from heat. Combine breadcrumbs and seasonings. Mix all ingredients together. Packaged stuffing mix may be substituted if you're in a rush

❧ Place a generous amount of stuffing on each piece of pork tenderloin. Roll up and wrap with a piece of bacon, securing with a toothpick. Place in a shallow casserole dish and bake at 300° F for approximately 1 ½ hours. Serve with baked potatoes.

Roasted Baron of Buffalo

Jean Hoare
Driftwillow Ranch, Stavely, Alberta

For years, Jean ran the famous Flying N Restaurant in Claresholm. A visit there was an all-evening affair as Jean spoiled her patrons with course after course of gourmet Western cuisine. She has graciously allowed us to use some of the recipes from her cookbooks.

When a couple of local ranchers began to stock buffalo, Jean decided to include the meat on her menu at the Flying N.

Buffalo can be used in any way that beef is used. The bones are heavier, the meat is darker and the fat usually has a yellow tinge, but other than that, it looks and behaves much like beef.

SERVES 8 TO 10

1   buffalo roast
       salt and freshly ground pepper

❧ Rub a mixture of salt and pepper over the roast. If it's very lean, wrap with extra suet, either buffalo or beef, which will baste the roast as it cooks.

❧ Roasting time can vary so greatly from one animal to another that it's safest to use a meat thermometer inserted into the thickest part of the roast. Don't let it touch the bone or the readings will be off. For rare, the thermometer should read 140 F, for medium 160 F and for well done 170 F. There will be less shrinkage if meat is roasted in a slow to moderate oven (275° to 325° F).

Buffalo Ribs

Jean Hoare
Driftwillow Ranch, Stavely, Alberta

    2 to 3 ribs per person (may substitute beef ribs)
1   package dry onion soup mix
    red wine

After several special dinners at Jean's restaurant featuring buffalo meat, she ended up with a lot of rib bones. They looked like they had possibilities, so she sawed them up, seared them quickly in a hot oven (450° F) to get them browned, then cooked the ribs slowly at 325° F for the next several hours.

As the ribs cooked, she sprinkled generous handfuls of dry onion soup mix over the bones and added about an inch of red wine. The ribs were turned as they browned on top.

After 2 to 3 hours of roasting, the wine had cooked down into a thick glaze and the meat was beautifully tender. Finger lickin' good!

Spiced Beef

Renie Blades
Rocking P Ranch, Nanton, Alberta

This recipe was given to Renie by her friend Jean Hoare, author of
Best Little Cookbook in the West. *With Jean's permission, here
is her Spiced Beef recipe.*

SERVES 20

5 lb	roast of beef (deer, elk, moose, buffalo may be substituted)
½ cup	Sifto quik-kure
½ cup	demerara sugar
3 tbsp	juniper berries
2 tbsp	ground allspice
2 tbsp	peppercorns
1 tsp	ground cloves
1 tsp	ground cinnamon
½ tsp	ground nutmeg
1 cup	cold water
— or —	
½ cup ea	cold water and maple syrup

❧ Pierce roast thoroughly on all surfaces with a sharp skewer
or knife. This will allow the spiced mixture to penetrate the
meat. In a large bowl, mix remaining ingredients and rub into
the roast, making sure all sides are coated. Place the meat and
spice mixture into a heavy plastic bag. Fasten the bag securely,
place in a bowl or pan that you will not need for 3 weeks. Store
overnight in refrigerator or in very cool spot.

ᨒ Next day, make sure all meat surfaces are moist and the spices are fairly evenly distributed. At least once a day, for three weeks, turn the bag over in the bowl for even-curing on all sides.

ᨒ After 3 weeks (give or take a day), remove meat from plastic bag, rinse under cold water, discarding the spices. Place meat in a roaster (if possible use a pan not much bigger than the meat). Add ¾ cup cold water and cover with a tight lid. Roast in a slow oven (275° F) for 4 hours. Then wrap meat in double thickness of foil and weigh it down for at least 12 hours. Turn meat over and weigh down on the other side for an additional 12 hours. Use at least 10 pounds of weight.

ᨒ Slice the pressed meat very thin and serve with horseradish in cream, pickled onions, spiced beets or fruit chutney.

Corned Beef

Ruth Pickett
Pickett Ranching Ltd., Bassano, Alberta

This is an old-time recipe that was popular when refrigeration wasn't available. The Picketts always made it at branding time. It was a favorite and fed a big crew.

SERVES A COUPLE OF HUNDRED ANYWAY

6 quarts	water
10 lbs	salt
8 lbs	sugar
1 tsp	saltpeter
100 lbs	beef

❧ Boil water and dissolve salt and sugar. Add saltpeter. This brine should be salty enough to float an egg. Put meat in a large stone crock (earthenware container) and add the brine. There should be enough brine to cover meat. Add more water, if necessary. Put a large plate on top and a rock or heavy weight to keep the meat covered.

❧ In 3 weeks, the meat should be cured enough to use. Dry meat and apply some liquid smoke, if desired. Wash meat well and boil until tender. This makes delicious corned beef sliced cold for sandwiches or hot with cabbage and potatoes.

Western Hash

Bill and Patricia Dunn
Mosquito Creek Ranch, Cayley, Alberta

Every rancher needs at least a hundred recipes that use ground beef.
Here's another one!

SERVES 4 TO 6

1 to 1 ½ lbs	ground beef
1	medium onion, chopped
1	28 oz can tomatoes
½ cup	celery or green pepper, chopped
½ cup	raw rice
	salt, pepper, oregano, basil to taste
1	14 oz can kernel corn, drained (optional)
1	14 oz can mushrooms, drained (optional)
	Cheddar or processed cheese (optional)

❧ Brown the beef. Add onions, tomatoes, celery or green pepper, rice and seasonings. Simmer 20 minutes, or until rice is tender. Add corn and mushrooms, if desired, and adjust seasonings. This is good served right out of a frying pan or piled into a casserole dish and topped with Cheddar or processed cheese.

Mr. and Mrs. Taco's Meatloaf Supreme

Cam and Jane Sutherland
High River, Alberta

Cam, or Taco as he is known, is a Canadian bullrider, CFR quali-fier and rancher. His wife, Jane Hawley, is a musician, songwriter, recording artist and performer. Jane's new CD is called Letters to Myself.

Jane says that the more she makes this meatloaf, the more ingre-dients she adds because every bullrider's style and taste is different. Isn't that the truth!

SERVES 4 REGULAR FOLKS OR 1 BULLRIDER

1 ¼ lbs	ground beef
½ cup	cracker crumbs
¼ cup	ketchup
¼ cup	barbecue sauce
	salt and pepper to taste
2 tsp	Worcestershire sauce
1	large onion, diced
1	10 oz can tomato soup
2 tsp	parsley flakes

❧ Combine all ingredients except tomato soup and parsley and pack into a meatloaf pan. Pour the tomato soup over the meat mixture and sprinkle with parsley. Cover pan tightly with foil. Bake at 375° F for 1 hour.

Cowgirl Casserole

Barb Poulsen
El Rancho Pequino, Claresholm, Alberta

A favorite with freshly baked buns and a tossed green salad.

SERVES 4 TO 6

1 lb	ground beef
1	medium onion, chopped
1	stalk celery, chopped
1	clove garlic, minced
½ cup	fresh mushrooms, sliced (optional)
1	14 oz can tomatoes
1 tbsp	honey
2 tsp	Italian seasoning or oregano
1 tsp	chili seasoning
	salt and pepper to taste
1 cup	Cheddar cheese, grated
— or —	
½ cup	processed cheese
4 to 6 oz	spaghetti, uncooked

❧ Brown ground beef, onion, celery, garlic and mushrooms. Add tomatoes, honey and seasonings. Simmer until flavors are well blended.

❧ In a casserole dish, layer spaghetti and sauce along with grated or processed cheese, ending with sauce. Bake in 350° F oven until spaghetti is tender.

Meat-Za Pie

Evelyn Livingstone
Val Terra Herefords, Vermilion, Alberta

A quick and easy supper dish. Add some buns and a salad and you've got a great meal!

SERVES 4 TO 6

1 lb	ground beef
½ cup	milk
⅓ cup	breadcrumbs or cracker crumbs
½ tsp	garlic salt
½ cup	ketchup
½ tsp	oregano
1	10 oz can mushroom pieces, drained
1 cup	Cheddar cheese, grated
	Parmesan cheese

Combine ground beef, milk, breadcrumbs and garlic salt and pat into a 9-inch pie plate to form a shell. In center of shell, place the rest of the ingredients in order. Bake at 375° F for 35 minutes. Sprinkle with Parmesan cheese.

Canadian Country Pie

Ann Britton
Flying Lazy B, Rokeby, Saskatchewan

A meal in itself, this dish needs only fresh buns or biscuits.

SERVES 4

3 tbsp	butter
2 cups	frozen hash brown potatoes
½ tsp	celery salt
¾ cup	fresh mushrooms, sliced
½ cup	onion, chopped
½ cup	green pepper, chopped
5	eggs
½ cup	milk
	salt and pepper to taste
1 cup	Cheddar cheese, grated
6	slices bacon, cooked crisp, crumbled

❧ In a frying pan, melt butter and sauté hash browns until brown and crusty, about 5 minutes. Sprinkle with celery salt and mix well. Spread evenly in a 9-inch pie plate. Top with mushrooms, onion and green pepper.

❧ Whisk together eggs, milk, salt and pepper and pour over top. Bake in a 350° F oven for 30 minutes, or until set. Remove from oven and sprinkle with Cheddar cheese and bacon. Put back in oven until cheese melts. Serve immediately.

Tourtière

David A. Poulsen
El Rancho Pequino, Claresholm, Alberta

David is a former rodeo competitor and clown who has become one of Canada's most sought-after rodeo announcers. An award-winning author, David's young adult novel Rodeo Trilogy *is in its second printing.*

Tourtière is a French-Canadian holiday dish traditionally served on Christmas Eve. It was first introduced to the Canadian West by fur-trading French Canadians during the 1860s. David and his wife, Barb, have adopted the tradition as their own.

MAKES 2 LARGE PIES

1 lb	ground beef
1 lb	ground pork
1	large onion, chopped
3	stalks celery, chopped
2	cloves garlic, minced
	water
1 large tbsp	honey
1 ½ cups	potatoes, cooked, mashed
— or —	
2 cups	bread, cubed
	salt and pepper to taste
2 tsp	ground allspice
2	unbaked double-crust pie shells

❧ Combine beef, pork, onion, garlic and celery in a large frying pan. Add water and cook until meat is no longer pink.

Drain most of the liquid, reserving about ⅔ cup. Add potatoes or bread cubes and other seasonings. Blend well.

❧ Pour mixture into prepared pie shells. Place top crusts over filling and make slits for steam to escape. Bake at 350° F for 30 to 45 minutes, or until pies are browned. This meat pie is excellent served with chutney, fresh buns and a green salad.

Enchiladas

Bonnie Gardner
Sentinel Ranch, Nanton, Alberta

Great with a tossed salad and a bottle of red wine!

SERVES 10 TO 12

2 lbs	ground beef
½ lb	ground pork
6	onions, chopped
2	28 oz cans tomato sauce
1 to 2 tsp	cumin
2 lbs	sharp Cheddar cheese, grated
2	small cans olives, chopped
24	large flour tortillas

❧ Brown meat and drain off fat. Boil onions and drain. Combine tomato sauce and cumin and heat to boiling. Mix half the tomato sauce with the meat. Add the onions, olives and half the cheese, reserving remaining cheese for topping.

❧ Dip tortillas in remaining sauce one at a time and lay on a plate. Fill each tortilla with about 2 tablespoons of filling and roll up. Lay rolled tortillas in a lightly greased casserole dish. Pour remaining sauce over tortillas and top with cheese. The casserole can be made to this point and frozen. When ready to eat, bake in a 325° F oven for 30 minutes. If frozen, bake for 1 hour.

Cheddar Lasagna

John and Kathy Duffy
Doubletree Ranch, Buck Lake, Alberta

Casseroles are great time savers and lasagna is especially popular for casual suppers. This recipe uses Cheddar rather than the traditional cottage cheese.

SERVES 4 TO 6

1 lb	ground beef
1	large onion, chopped
1	clove garlic, chopped
1 tsp	parsley flakes
2	bay leaves
1 tsp	salt
½ tsp	black pepper
½ tsp	oregano
½ tsp	basil
¼ tsp	thyme
1	28 oz can tomatoes, diced
1	14 oz can tomato sauce
1	10 oz can mushrooms, sliced
1	large green pepper, diced
2	stalks celery, diced
1	jalapeno pepper, diced
10 to 12	lasagna noodles
2 cups	Cheddar cheese, grated
1 cup	mozzarella cheese, grated

❧ Brown meat and cook onion and garlic. Add remaining ingredients except noodles and cheeses and heat thoroughly, simmering until desired consistency, approximately 1 hour.

❧ Cook noodles according to package directions. Spray a 9 x 13-inch lasagna pan with nonstick cooking spray, cover the bottom with noodles. Pour in half the meat sauce, add another layer of noodles and the remaining meat sauce. Top with grated cheeses. Bake in 325° F oven for 25 minutes. Broil 3 to 5 minutes, or until surface is browned. Allow to sit 15 minutes before serving.

Gourmet Hot Dogs

Ian and Twylla Tyson
Ian Tyson Cutting Horses, Longview, Alberta

Both children and adults like this simple, easy-to-make dish.

SERVES 6 TO 8

12	good quality wieners or smokies
12	hot dog buns
	ketchup
	mayonnaise
	mustard
	Cheddar cheese, grated
	green onion, chopped
	tomato, chopped

❧ Boil or microwave wieners until almost done. Split buns apart and spread each one with ketchup, mayonnaise and mustard. Split wieners in half and place on buns. Top with grated cheese, onion and tomato. Put under broiler and broil until cheese melts. Serve with olives and green chiles.

Dunkin' Wieners

Jay and Wendy Lundy
O7 Cattle Co., Medicine Hat, Alberta

This dish is quick and easy to prepare, whether on the range, trail rides or at brandings. Everyone loves it, especially when served with sourdough biscuits and baked beans.

SERVES 4

2 cups	onion, chopped
¼ cup	oil
1 ¼ cups	ketchup
½ cup	water
¼ cup	brown sugar
1 tbsp	vinegar
2 tbsp	Worcestershire sauce
½ tsp	dry mustard
1 tsp	salt
1 lb	wieners, chopped

Cook onions in oil until tender. Add remaining ingredients. Simmer until wieners are tender.

Aussie Burgers

Bernie and Dawn Smyth
Red Roo Ranch, Medicine Hat, Alberta

Former Australian and Canadian All-Around Champion Cowboy, Bernie claims this is a popular Australian dish at barbecues, brandings and rodeos.

SERVES 1

1 to 2	slices bacon, cooked crisp
1	beef patty
1	egg
1	hamburger bun
	mayonnaise
	beets slices
	tomato slices
	pineapple rings
	cheese slice
	lettuce

🍂 Cook bacon, beef patty and egg. Assemble all ingredients in order of choice on hamburger bun. Enjoy!

Barbecued Beef on a Bun

Bonnie Gardner
Sentinel Ranch, Nanton, Alberta

Bonnie picked up this recipe years ago when she worked in the four-corners area of Colorado. It came from the wife of a pinto bean farmer-rancher and has become a popular choice at branding time. The recipe can be doubled or tripled, depending on appetites and other dishes being served.

SERVES 12 TO 15

4 lbs	chuck roast (or any other tough cut of beef)
2	medium onions, chopped
¼ cup	butter
2 cups	ketchup
2 tbsp	vinegar
2 tbsp	Worcestershire sauce
1 tbsp	salt
½ tsp	cayenne
½ tsp	black pepper
1 tsp	chili powder
1 cup	beef broth

&. Place roast in cast iron Dutch oven with lid and cook in slow oven (300° F) until meat shreds easily with fork. Brown onions in butter. Add remaining ingredients and simmer 2 hours. Serve over buns.

Chicken Salad Sandwiches

Helen Giles
Giles Ranches, High River, Alberta

This recipe makes a delicious sandwich filling and is a good way to use up leftover chicken or turkey.

SERVES 12

2 ½ cups	cooked chicken, cubed
4	hard-boiled eggs, diced
¾ cup	salad dressing
2 ½ cups	celery, finely diced
1 tsp	salt
	dash lemon pepper and paprika
1 ½ cups	tart apple, finely chopped
1 tbsp	lemon juice
¼ cup	butter
	lettuce (optional)

❧ Mix all ingredients well, then spread on sliced bread of your choice.

Chicken-in-the-Gold

Jean Hoare
Driftwillow Ranch, Stavely, Alberta

SERVES 4

The curry sauce adds a touch of India to this tasty dish.

2	2 ½ to 3 lb chickens, halved
1 cup	honey
1 cup	prepared mustard
1 tbsp	curry powder
	orange slices and parsley for garnish

🍃 Precook chicken. Prepare the sauce by heating together honey, mustard and curry powder. Reheat chicken until hot throughout but not browned. Brush underside of chicken with sauce and place under broiler until brown and bubbling. Turn and generously brush sauce on other side. Broil again until brown and bubbling. Watch carefully at this point as the honey will brown very quickly. You want gold, not burnt offerings. Garnish with orange slices and parsley. Serve with rice or roasted potatoes.

Salmon Harvest Casserole

Helen Giles
Giles Ranches, High River, Alberta

A good casserole to take to the field for hungry harvesters.

SERVES 4 TO 6 VERY GENEROUSLY

3	7 oz cans salmon
1 ½ cups	elbow macaroni, uncooked
1	12 oz can kernel corn, drained
1	large tomato, diced
4	green onions, chopped
½ cup	green pepper or celery, diced
1	10 oz can cream of celery soup
— or —	
2 cups	white sauce (recipe next page)
2 tbsp	lemon juice
½ tsp	salt
¼ tsp	pepper
3 oz	processed cheese, cubed

🍃 Drain salmon, reserving juice. Break salmon into chunks. Cook macaroni until tender, then drain. Layer macaroni in a large casserole dish. Distribute salmon over macaroni, then add corn, tomato, onion and green pepper or celery. Combine salmon juice and soup. Add remaining ingredients except cheese. Pour over casserole and stir gently. Bake, uncovered, at 375° F for 20 to 25 minutes. Sprinkle cheese over top and continue baking until cheese is melted.

White Sauce

This sauce gives a nice flavor to any fish dish.

4 tbsp	melted shortening
4 tbsp	flour
2 cups	milk
	salt and pepper to taste

❧ Melt shortening in a saucepan. Add flour, salt and pepper, stirring to form smooth paste. Add milk, stirring constantly, until sauce is thick and creamy.

Seafood Chowder

Bill and Pearl Collins
Leecoll Stables Ltd., Calgary, Alberta

Bill Collins was a four-time Canadian Calf Roping Champion and is one of Canada's premiere cutting horse trainers and competitors. He has been inducted into the Canadian Rodeo Hall of Fame as well as the Canadian and National Cutting Horse Halls of Fame. Bill received the Order of Canada in 1996.

SERVES 4 TO 6

3 tbsp	butter
1	onion, diced
4	medium potatoes, peeled, diced
1	halibut steak
1	16 oz can clams and juice
1	14 oz can evaporated milk
	salt, pepper, garlic powder and fish seasoning to taste

&. Melt butter in a saucepan and sauté onions for 1 minute. Add potatoes and enough water to cover. Simmer until potatoes are half done. Lay halibut steak on top of potatoes and simmer until fish flakes away easily from the bone. Remove bone and skin from the fish. Add remaining ingredients and heat but do not boil. If chowder is too thick, add regular milk to thin.

[Snacks & Desserts]

Mother's Great Rolled-Oat Cookies

Renie Blades
Rocking P Ranch, Nanton, Alberta

When Renie's kids were small, they often rode over to Grandma Blades to visit and eat her rolled oat cookies. This recipe actually comes not from Grandma Blades but from her mother, Laura Macleary.

MAKES 2 DOZEN COOKIES

½ cup	butter
1 cup	brown sugar
1	egg, lightly beaten
1 cup	flour
1 tsp	baking soda
1 tsp	baking powder
¼ tsp	salt
1 tsp	vanilla
¾ cup	coconut
2 ½ cups	rolled oats
½ cup	raisins (optional)

✄ Mix butter, brown sugar and egg. Add dry ingredients and roll mixture into small balls. Flatten with a fork on a cookie sheet. Bake at 325° F for 10 minutes. This recipe doubles very well.

Old-Fashioned Ginger Cookies

Ruth Pickett
Pickett Ranching Ltd., Bassano, Alberta

These cookies are a favorite mid-morning snack, especially after rising at 4:30 in the morning to gather the herd.

MAKES 8 DOZEN COOKIES

1 cup	butter
1 ½ cups	honey
1 cup	molasses
¼ cup	hot water
2 tsp	ground ginger
1 tsp	ground cinnamon
1 tsp	salt
2 tbsp	vinegar
2 tsp	baking soda
2	eggs
4 to 5 cups	flour

⟋ In a saucepan, combine all ingredients except soda, eggs and flour. Heat, then cool slightly. Add remaining ingredients. Mix together well and chill in refrigerator for a couple of hours.

⟋ Break off small amounts of dough and roll in sugar. Place on cookie sheet and press down slightly on each cookie with a fork dipped in sugar. Bake at 325° F for 12 to 15 minutes.

Scratch-My-Back Cookies

Bill and Pearl Collins
Leecoll Stables, Calgary, Alberta

These cookies were Pearl's Grandmother Harrington's favorite.

MAKES 2 DOZEN COOKIES

¾ cup	butter
1 cup	brown sugar
1	egg
1 ¼ cups	flour
½ tsp	salt
1 tsp	vanilla
½ tsp	baking soda
1 cup	rolled oats
1 cup	coconut

❧ Mix butter, sugar and egg. Add remaining ingredients. Drop by teaspoonfuls onto cookie sheet and bake at 350° F for 10 to 15 minutes.

Mexican Wedding-Cake Cookies

Shirley Armstrong
Bow Cattle Co., Bassano, Alberta

Not actually a cake but cookies instead, this treasure was given to Shirley's mother, Billie Burrows, by her friend Alice Hyrve. Both ladies are now in their 90s. Shirley's mother, though nearly blind, still makes this recipe for afternoon tea.

MAKES 4 DOZEN COOKIES

1 cup	butter
½ cup	berry sugar
2 cups	flour
1 cup	pecans or walnuts, finely ground
¼ tsp	salt
1 tsp	vanilla

❧ Cream softened butter and sugar. Add remaining ingredients and mix well. Form into small crescent shapes and bake at 350° F for 15 minutes. Roll in icing sugar when cooled. These cookies will melt in your mouth.

Fruit Punch Bars

Peggy Herman
Herman's Horned Herefords, Bindloss, Alberta

This recipe is great for 4-H get-togethers or field days.

MAKES 12 BARS

2	eggs
1 ½ cup	sugar
1	14 oz tin fruit cocktail, drained
2 ¼ cup	flour
½ tsp	soda
1 tsp	vanilla
½ cup	walnuts
1 ½ cup	coconut
¾ cup	sugar
½ cup	butter
¼ cup	cream
½ tsp	vanilla

❧ Grease and flour a cookie sheet. Beat eggs and sugar at high speed until light. Add fruit cocktail, flour, soda and vanilla. Beat at medium speed until well blended. Turn batter into pan. Sprinkle with nuts and coconut. Bake in 350° F oven for 25 minutes.

❧ Boil sugar, butter, cream and vanilla in a saucepan for two minutes, stirring constantly. Cool slightly and pour over batter. Cut into bars.

Flapjack

Barbara Hughes
Chinook Ranch, Longview, Alberta

This is a family favorite that Barb used to have as an afternoon treat at her grannie's house in England. Her own children are great fans!

SERVES 10 TO 12

½ cup	butter
scant ½ cup	brown sugar
3 tbsp	treacle (Roger's Golden Syrup)
3 cups	rolled oats
½ tsp	salt

ᨆ Melt butter, sugar and treacle, then add rolled oats and salt. Mix well. Bake in a greased 8 x 8-inch pan at 350° F for 25 minutes, or until golden brown. Cut into squares while hot.

Farmer's Brownies

Peggy Herman
Herman's Horned Herefords, Bindloss, Alberta

Brownies first became popular during the 1920s. They remain just as popular today and are a good dessert to take to community suppers.

MAKES 12 BROWNIES

¼ cup	cocoa
1 cup	hot water
¾ cup	butter
2 cups	sugar
2	eggs
2 ½ cups	flour
1 tsp	baking soda
½ tsp	salt
½ cup	sour milk or buttermilk
1 tsp	vanilla
1 cup	chopped nuts

ꝫ Mix cocoa and hot water and let cool. Cream butter and sugar. Add eggs and beat well. Sift dry ingredients and add to creamed mixture. Add cocoa, buttermilk and vanilla. Mix well. Add nuts. Spread on greased cookie sheet and bake in a 375° F oven for 20 minutes. When cool, ice with a chocolate butter icing (recipe page 295) or make a chocolate sauce (recipe page 312) and pour over top.

Victoria Sandwich

Barbara Hughes
Chinook Ranch, Longview, Alberta

This was Barb's mother's favorite birthday cake when she was a little girl in England. It's simple to make and easy to transport.

SERVES 12 TO 16

4	eggs, well beaten
1 ½ cups	sugar
½ lb	butter
2 cups	flour
1 tsp	salt
	raspberry jam

❧ Beat butter to cream and dredge in flour and sugar. Add eggs. Pour into a lightly greased flat pan and bake at 350° F for 20 to 30 minutes. For a thicker cake use a deeper pan.

❧ When cold, slice horizontally and spread layers with raspberry jam. Place layers together and sprinkle top with icing sugar. Cut into squares.

Plum Kuchen

Sharon MacDonald Burton
Victoria, British Columbia

This recipe takes advantage of plums at their best.

SERVES 6 TO 8

½ cup	butter
1 cup	sugar
1	egg
½ cup	sour cream
¼ tsp	vanilla
1 cup	flour
½ tsp	baking powder
¼ tsp	salt
1 lb	fresh plums
¼ cup	sugar
½ heaping tsp	ground cinnamon

❧ Cream butter and sugar. Add egg and beat until fluffy. Stir in sour cream and vanilla. Sift together flour, baking powder and salt. Fold into batter just until moistened. Spread batter in a greased and floured 9-inch layer cake pan or a 9-inch square pan. Wash and quarter plums. Do not peel. Arrange plums on top. Combine sugar and cinnamon and sprinkle over plums.

❧ Bake at 350° F for 50 to 60 minutes. Cut into wedges and serve with ice cream or whipped cream. During baking, watch that bottom of kuchen doesn't burn.

Orange Pudding

Helen Gilchrist
Cypress Cattle Co., Maple Creek, Saskatchewan

This was a popular dessert with Mom Gilchrist when she cooked for ranch hands. Double the recipe for large crowds.

SERVES 6

1	egg, beaten
1 cup	sugar
1 cup	water
1 heaping tbsp	flour
4 to 6	oranges, peeled, cut into wedges

Boil first 4 ingredients until thick, stirring often. Cool and pour over oranges. At Christmas, add green and red cherries for a festive touch!

Mrs. Mac's Rice Pudding

Vivian MacDonald
Salmon Arm, British Columbia

This is a creamy, nourishing pudding, great hot or cold with cinnamon and cream poured over top. It's been a favorite with every generation of MacDonalds.

SERVES 4 TO 6

2 cups	water
½ cup	long grained rice
1 ½ cups	milk
½ cup	sugar
1	egg
	pinch of salt
½ cup	raisins
	cream and cinnamon

❧ Heat water in double boiler or heavy saucepan. Add rice and boil until almost dry. Add milk and sugar. Simmer until rice is soft. Beat egg and add, stirring quickly. Add salt and raisins. Stir and set aside. Pudding will thicken as it cools. Serve with a bit of cream poured over top and a dusting of cinnamon.

Steamed Pudding (Duff and Dip)

Chuckwagon cooks used to serve this as a special treat for cowboys out on the range. Try it with plum pudding sauce (recipe next page).

SERVES 4 TO 6

1 ½ cups	flour
½ tsp	baking soda
¼ tsp	salt
1 tsp	ground cinnamon
¼ tsp	ground cloves
½ tsp	ground nutmeg
¼ tsp	ground ginger
½ cup	shortening
½ cup	raisins, dates or chopped apple
⅔ cup	milk
½ cup	light molasses

❧ Combine dry ingredients. Work shortening in well. Add fruit, then milk and molasses. Mix well. Spoon into a glass bowl or pudding mold. Cover with foil and tie foil securely with string. Place bowl on metal ring or trivet in a large pot with 2 to 3 inches of water in bottom. Cover pot and steam pudding for 2 to 3 hours.

Plum Pudding Sauce

Shirley Armstrong
Bow Cattle Co., Bassano, Alberta

This recipe was Shirley's grandmother's recipe. Teresa Fulton, originally from New York, made her way to Alberta in the early 1900s. While we're used to exact measurements when we cook today, cooking was much less exact in the early part of the century, hence the following measurement for butter.

SERVES 8 TO 10

	butter the size of an egg
2 cups	icing sugar
2	eggs, separated
	vanilla
½ cup	milk

🍐 Cream butter and sugar, then add egg yolks and milk. Beat well. Heat in double boiler just enough to melt. Just before serving, add vanilla and beaten egg whites. This is enough sauce for a large steamed pudding.

Boozy Pudding

Kim Hitchner
Longview, Alberta

This is a variation of traditional English trifle.

SERVES 8

¼ cup	alcohol (rum, brandy or sherry)
1	package ladyfingers
2	packages vanilla dessert topping mix
1 cup	milk
¾ cup	water
¼ cup	alcohol
1 cup	whipping cream, whipped

❧ Sprinkle ladyfingers with alcohol of your choice. Mix dessert topping with milk according to package directions. Add water and remaining ¼ cup of alcohol.

❧ Line springform pan or glass bowl with ladyfingers, standing them on end. Pour pudding mixture into the center of bowl. Cover with whipped cream. For variation, try sprinkling with nuts, grated chocolate or cherries.

Baked Custard

V.E. Hanson
Calgary, Alberta

A simple, easy dessert to prepare. Great with sliced strawberries on top.

SERVES 4 TO 6

5	eggs, beaten
1 ½ cups	sugar
1 tsp	cornstarch
4 cups	milk
½ tsp	salt

❧ Beat eggs well. Add sugar. Blend well. Add remaining ingredients, then pour mixture into a buttered casserole dish. Place dish in a pan of water and bake for 1 hour in a 350° F oven.

Prince of Wales Cake

Jean Hoare
Driftwillow Ranch, Stavely, Alberta

This recipe is named for the Prince of Wales, who, in 1919, purchased a ranch in southern Alberta known as the EP Ranch.

SERVES 12 TO 16

2 cups	raisins
2 ½ cups	water
1 cup	butter or oil
2 cups	brown sugar
2	eggs
1 tsp	vanilla
2 ½ cups	flour
2 tsp	baking soda
1 tsp	baking powder
2 tsp	ground cinnamon
2 tsp	ground nutmeg
1 tsp	salt

🍂 Simmer the raisins and water for 10 minutes. Cool and drain, reserving the liquid.

🍂 Mix butter or oil, sugar, eggs and vanilla. Add reserved liquid. Sift the dry ingredients together and add to the first mixture. Stir well. Fold in the raisins. Pour into a greased and floured 9 x 13-inch cake pan and bake at 350° F for about 40 minutes, or until a cake tester comes out clean when inserted into the center of the cake. When cool, frost with icing (recipe next page).

Eva's Dimple Icing

2 cups	brown sugar, packed
¾ cup	cream, sweet or sour
1 tbsp	butter
1 tbsp	vanilla

❧ In a fairly heavy pot, mix together sugar and cream. Bring to a boil, stirring, and continue cooking for about 8 to 10 minutes, or until the soft ball stage is reached (236° F on a candy thermometer or when a bit of the mixture forms a soft ball when dropped into cold water). Remove from heat, add butter and vanilla. Beat until sticky but still shiny. Take care, as this can harden quickly. Spread over the cake before it hardens completely.

❧ If you've been overly generous with the cream or the icing does not turn creamy and thick, gradually add some sifted icing sugar until the mixture is of spreading consistency. The flavor won't be quite as wonderful, but close.

Mom's Chocolate-Sour Cream Cake

Peggy Herman
Herman's Horned Herefords, Bindloss, Alberta

Peggy's mom made this every Sunday for their ropings.

SERVES 12 TO 16

⅓ cup	cocoa
⅓ cup	boiling water
2 or 3	eggs, beaten
1 ½ cups	sour cream
1 ¾ cups	sugar
1 tsp	vanilla
2 cups	flour
½ tsp	baking powder
1 ½ tsp	baking soda
½ tsp	salt

🍂 Mix together cocoa and boiling water. Set aside. Beat eggs, sour cream, sugar and vanilla. Sift together flour, baking powder, baking soda and salt. Add to egg mixture, beating well after each addition. Add cocoa and boiling water and beat well. Pour into a greased and floured 9 x 13-inch cake pan. Bake in a 350° F oven for 30 to 35 minutes.

Burnt Sugar Cake

Cheryl Livingstone
Val Terra Herefords, Vermilion, Alberta

This cake was a very popular dessert recipe years ago. It was taken to community card parties and dances. It was also one of Cheryl's favorite childhood recipes and one she makes today when she caters parties and needs a variety of cakes.

SERVES 12 TO 14

1 cup	sugar
1 cup	boiling water
2 cups	cake flour
— or —	
1 ¾ cups	all-purpose flour
2 tsp	baking powder
½ tsp	salt
½ cup	butter
2	eggs
1 tsp	vanilla

&. Grease and flour two layer cake pans or one 9 x 13-inch pan. Place ½ cup sugar in a heavy saucepan, stirring constantly until sugar melts and browns (caramelizes). Remove from heat and add boiling water. Stir until sugar is dissolved. Cool.

&. Sift together flour, baking powder and salt. Cream butter with other ½ cup sugar until fluffy. Add eggs, then beat thoroughly until mixture is light and sugar is dissolved. Add vanilla. Add the dry ingredients and caramelized sugar alternately in three parts. Mix well. Pour into prepared pans and bake at 350° F. Layer cake pans will require 20 to 25 minutes, while a 9 x 13-inch pan will take a bit longer. Frost with sweetened whipped cream or caramel icing (recipe page 287).

Easy Cake

Bill and Pearl Collins
Leecoll Stables Ltd, Calgary, Alberta

As the name says, this is an easy, versatile cake that can be served iced, plain or with chocolate sauce (recipe page 312) and nuts on top.

SERVES 8 TO 10

¼ cup	butter
2	eggs, beaten
	milk
1 cup	flour
1 cup	sugar
1 tsp	baking powder
½ tsp	salt
1 tsp	vanilla

❧ Melt butter in a saucepan, then add beaten eggs and enough milk to equal 1 cup. Transfer to a bowl and add remaining ingredients. Mix well and bake in a greased 8 x 8-inch pan at 350° F until done.

Diana's Rhubarb Cake

Don and Joyce Ulrich
Ulrich Polled Herefords, Medicine Hat, Alberta

SERVES 12 TO 14

Cake

1 ½ cups	white sugar
½ cups	butter
1	egg, beaten
1 tsp	baking soda
2 cups	flour
1 tsp	ground cinnamon
¾ tsp	salt
1 cup	sour milk or buttermilk
1 tsp	vanilla
2 cups	rhubarb, chopped

Topping

½ cup	butter
½ cup	brown sugar
½ cup	coconut

❧ Cream sugar and butter. Add egg, then sift dry ingredients together and add alternately with sour milk. Milk may be soured by adding 1 tablespoon of vinegar to 1 cup of milk. Stir in vanilla and rhubarb last. Bake at 350° F for 45 minutes.

❧ To make topping, mix butter, sugar and coconut, then spread on top of cooled cake. Return to oven to brown.

Green Apple Cake

Jeannine Lewis
Okotoks, Alberta

SERVES 10 TO 12

2	eggs
¾ cup	oil
2 cups	sugar
2 tsp	vanilla
2 cups	flour
1 tsp	baking soda
½ tsp	salt
2 tsp	ground cinnamon
5	green apples

❧ Beat eggs and oil until well mixed. Add remaining ingredients except apples and mix well. Peel apples and slice thinly. Add to flour mixture. Mix well. Bake at 350° F for 45 minutes. Frost when cool with cream cheese icing (recipe below).

Cream Cheese Icing

8 oz	cream cheese
3 tsp	butter
2 tsp	vanilla
2 cups	icing sugar

❧ Blend all ingredients together. Spread on cooled cake.

Never-Fail Chocolate Cake

Vivian MacDonald
Salmon Arm, British Columbia

As the name says, this cake never fails. It's been a staple in the Mac-Donald family for years and is quick to throw together for unexpected company. The measurement for butter was a common way to describe ingredient measurements years ago.

SERVES 8 TO 10

¾ cup	white sugar
1	egg
	butter the size of an egg
¼ cup	sour milk or buttermilk
4 tsp	cocoa
1 tsp	baking soda
1 tsp	baking powder
1 cup	flour
¼ cup	boiling water

❧ Cream sugar, egg and butter. Add sour milk. Milk may be soured by adding 1 tablespoon of vinegar to 1 cup of milk. Combine dry ingredients and add to sugar-egg mixture. Mix until well blended. Add boiling water and beat. Pour into a greased 9-inch pan. Bake for 25 to 30 minutes in 350° F oven. Frost with icing when cool (recipe next page).

Chocolate Butter Icing

1 cup	icing sugar
1 heaping tbsp	cocoa
3 tbsp	butter
	milk

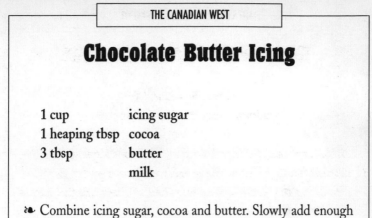 Combine icing sugar, cocoa and butter. Slowly add enough milk until mixture is smooth. Spread on cooled cake.

Crumb Cake

Patricia and Bill Dunn
Mosquito Creek Ranch, Cayley, Alberta

This pre-1900 heritage recipe is easy to make. It's a favorite for coffee, lunch or to take out to the fields.

SERVES 10 TO 12

2 cups	flour
1 cup	white sugar
¾ cup	butter
1 tsp	baking soda
1 tsp	ground cloves
1 tsp	ground cinnamon
1 cup	raisins
1 cup	sour milk or buttermilk
1	egg, beaten

❧ Mix flour, sugar and butter to form a crumb-like mixture. Set 1 cup of this aside for topping.

❧ Add remaining ingredients to rest of crumbs. (Please note that milk may be soured by adding 1 tablespoon of vinegar to 1 cup of milk.) Pour mixture into a greased 9-inch pan. Sprinkle reserved crumbs on top and pat down gently. Bake at 350° F for about 40 minutes, or until cake tests done when toothpick inserted in center comes out clean.

Apple Streusel Cheesecake

Allana Annett and April Beckley
Three Bars Cattle and Guest Ranch,
Cranbrook, British Columbia

This decadent dessert is another of the Three Bars Ranch recipes that return clients often request.

SERVES 10

½ cup	butter
½ cup	white sugar
1 cup	flour
3	apples, peeled and sliced
¼ cup	white sugar
2 tbsp	butter
2 tbsp	milk or water
1 cup	cream cheese, softened
½ cup	brown sugar, firmly packed
2	eggs
1 cup	sour cream
2 tbsp	lemon juice
½ cup	flour
¼ cup	brown sugar, firmly packed
¼ tsp	ground cinnamon
¼ cup	butter, softened

❧ Cream butter and sugar. Add flour and blend. Press into the bottom and ½ inch up the side of a greased 9-inch springform pan. Bake 12 to 15 minutes at 350° F.

⁂ Combine apples, sugar, butter and milk in a saucepan and cook until apples are tender. Drain apples and place in the bottom of cooled crust.

⁂ Beat cream cheese and sugar until smooth. Add eggs, sour cream and lemon juice. Mix well. Pour this mixture over apples.

⁂ Combine remaining ingredients and mix until crumbly. Sprinkle over cream cheese mixture. Bake 45 to 60 minutes at 350° F, or until a knife inserted in center of cake comes out clean. Chill at least 4 hours, or overnight. This dessert freezes well for up to 3 months.

Lemon Cheesecake

Judy Lucas
Lucasia Ranch, Claresholm, Alberta

This recipe often finds its way to neighborhood get-togethers and brandings in the Porcupine Hills.

SERVES 12

1 box	vanilla biscuits, crumbled
— or —	
3 cups	graham wafer crumbs
2 tbsp	melted butter
½ cup	sugar
1 cup	boiling water
1	small package lemon Jell-O
8 oz	cream cheese
1 cup	sugar
1	14 oz can 2% evaporated milk (well chilled)
1 tsp	lemon juice

☙ Mix crumbs with melted butter and sugar. Pat into a large cake pan. Mix boiling water and Jell-O and let stand until thick.

☙ Beat cream cheese with sugar. Beat evaporated milk and lemon juice, then blend into cream cheese mixture. Add thickened Jell-O. Pour mixture over crumbs and chill thoroughly.

Macadamia Nut Cheesecake

Jeannine Lewis
Okotoks, Alberta

*Jeannine is the daughter of Royal Burrows, a horseman, rancher
and former Canadian Cutting Horse Champion. Jeannine has
spent most of her life ranching, raising Brahma cattle and horses
and following the rodeo trail with her kids.*

SERVES 10 TO 12

¼ cup	butter
¼ cup	brown sugar
1 cup	flour
½ cup	macadamia nuts, crushed
8 oz	cream cheese
½ cup	sugar
1 tsp	vanilla
1 cup	whipping cream

🍂 Mix together the butter, sugar, flour and nuts to make crust.
Spread evenly on a cookie sheet. Cook 15 minutes at 350° F,
or until golden brown. While still hot, crumble with a fork and
mold into pie pan.

🍂 Combine cream cheese, sugar and vanilla and beat until
smooth. Whip cream until stiff. Fold cream cheese into
whipped cream. Spread filling into cooled pie crust. Chill 1
hour before serving. Scatter some additional crushed
macadamia nuts over top before serving. Delicious!

Boston Cream Pie

Steve Dunham
Dunham Training Stables, Turner Valley, Alberta

Former Canadian Bareback and All-Around Champion, Steve is currently one of Canada's top rope and stock horse trainers. His mom, Fay, says that he doesn't actually bake this pie himself, but he does like to eat it.

SERVES 10 TO 12

Batter

3	eggs
¼ cup	milk
1 cup	sugar
1 ⅔ cups	flour, sifted
2 tsp	baking powder
½ tsp	salt

Filling

1 cup	milk
3 tbsp	flour
¼ cup	sugar
⅛ tsp	salt
1	egg, beaten
1 tbsp	butter
½ tsp	vanilla

❧ Beat eggs until light and foamy. Gradually beat in milk and sugar. Continue beating until thick and light. Mix dry ingredients. Gradually sift or sprinkle dry ingredients over egg mixture, folding in with a spatula.

❧ Divide batter between 2 greased 8-inch layer cake pans. Bake in preheated 350° F oven for 25 to 30 minutes.

❧ To make filling, scald milk in top of a double boiler. Combine flour, sugar and salt. Gradually add some of the hot milk to flour mixture and blend until smooth. Stir flour mixture into remaining hot milk and cook in a double boiler over medium heat until mixture comes to a boil, stirring constantly.

❧ Remove from heat and stir part of hot mixture into beaten egg. Return to double boiler and cook another 2 minutes, stirring constantly. Remove from heat, cool slightly, then stir in butter and vanilla. Cool and spread on cake between layers. Serve with favorite topping. Steve's favorite is chocolate fudge icing drizzled over top. Chill in refrigerator before serving.

Bullrider Pie

Well, no, that's not what it's really called, but when you hear the story you'll understand why someone might hang that name on it. When 1988 Canadian Bull Riding Champion Dan Lowry was living in Edmonton, Alberta, he made his laundry facilities available to his neighbor and soon-to-be country music star Jane Hawley. One night Jane decided to combine a laundry expedition to Dan's house with a little spying mission. Dan's girl friend was out of town, and Jane assumed that because no bull rider could be trusted, Dan might just be entertaining someone else that evening. After a well-executed sneak-up on Dan's house, Jane raced up onto the darkened porch and banged on the door, convinced she would catch the shocked and dismayed Mr. Lowry in the act. In fact, Dan was shocked and dismayed. But his concern wasn't at being caught. In fact, there was no girl. His cry, "My pies, my pies!" told the story. Dan's freshly baked rhubarb pies were in the porch cooling, and Dan was distraught at the prospect that Jane, in her stealth, may have inadvertently stepped on one. The pies survived and Jane got over her suspicion of bull riders, later marrying one of her own, Cam Sutherland. Dan's famous rhubarb pie recipe—for which he credits Betty Crocker as his inspiration—follows.

Dan's Rhubarb Pie

Dan Lowry
Valleyview, Alberta

SERVES 6 TO 8

2 ½ cups	rhubarb, chopped
1 cup	sugar
2	eggs, lightly beaten
1	unbaked double-crust pie shell

❧ Combine rhubarb, sugar and beaten eggs in a large bowl.

❧ Prepare pie crust. When rolling out crust, it is not necessary to follow Dan's example as he admits that his method involves piecing together the pie crust in roughly 2-inch pieces!

❧ Pour filling into pie crust. Cover with top crust. Sprinkle sugar on top. Bake at 400° F for 10 minutes, until crust starts to brown, then for 30 minutes more at 350° F, or until rhubarb is soft.

Fay's Apple Pie

Fay Dunham
Dunham Training Stables, Turner Valley, Alberta

SERVES 6 TO 8

Pastry

2 cups	flour
⅔ cup	lard
½ tsp	salt
¼ tsp	baking powder
½ tsp	sugar

Filling

6	apples, peeled, sliced
1 to 1 ½ cups	sugar
1 tsp	ground cinnamon

🍂 Blend with pastry blender until mixture resembles corn-meal. Toss with several tablespoons of cold water or cold milk just enough to moisten. Roll out pastry and place in a large pie plate. Brush with melted butter.

🍂 Slice apples into a bowl and toss with sugar and cinnamon. Arrange in pie crust and dot with butter. Brush crust edge with milk, then add top crust. Crimp edges and cut a small, round hole in center of top crust. Push apples aside to bottom crust. This stops pie from boiling over. Cut decorative steam vents in top of pie. Bake at 375° F for 50 minutes, or until golden brown and apples are tender.

Paper-Sack Apple Pie

Bonnie Gardner
Sentinel Ranch, Nanton, Alberta

The crumb topping makes this a "lighter" pie. Baked in a paper sack or bag, the pie is less likely to burn while cooking.

SERVES 6 TO 8

3 to 4	large apples
½ cup	sugar
½ tsp	ground nutmeg
2 tbsp	flour
1 to 2 tbsp	lemon juice
	dash of salt
½ cup	brown sugar
½ cup	flour
¼ to ½ cup	butter
1	unbaked single-crust pie shell

🍃 Peel and slice apples. Combine sugar, nutmeg and 2 table-spoons flour. Sprinkle over apples and coat well. Spoon this mixture into unbaked pie shell. Sprinkle with lemon juice and add a dash of salt. Combine brown sugar, ½ cup flour and butter. Blend well and sprinkle over top of pie. Place in large brown paper bag and secure with clips. Bake at 425° F for 1 hour.

Carrot Pie

Lauren Hitchner
Hitchner Quarter Horses, Longview, Alberta

On the eastern slopes of the Rocky Mountains the climate does not often allow people to grow pumpkins, so ranch cooks have adapted the pumpkin pie recipe to make use of carrots. Carrots grow in abundance and produce a superior "pumpkin" pie with a rich flavor and pleasing color.

SERVES 18

4 cups	cooked carrots, pureed
3	eggs, beaten
3 cups	hot milk
1 ½ cups	brown sugar
2 tsp	ground cinnamon
½ tsp	ground cloves
½ tsp	ground ginger
1 tsp	salt
3	unbaked single-crust pie shells

❧ Puree cooked carrots in food processor. Beat eggs well. Gradually add hot milk to beaten eggs, then add remaining ingredients, mixing well with electric beater.

❧ Pour into prepared unbaked pie shells and bake in a 350° F oven until set and puffy. Test doneness by inserting knife into center. If knife comes out clean, custard is done. Serve with whipped cream and sprinkle with cinnamon.

Saskatoon Glaze Pie

As huckleberries are to Montana and Idaho, saskatoons are to Alberta and Saskatchewan.

Serves 6 to 8

4 cups	fresh saskatoons
1 ½ cups	mashed saskatoons
1 cup	sugar
1 tbsp	cornstarch
⅛ tsp	salt
1 tbsp	lemon juice
1	unbaked single-crust pie shell

❧ Place fresh saskatoons in bottom of an uncooked pie shell. Combine mashed saskatoons in a saucepan with sugar, cornstarch and salt. Bring to a boil and cook 1 minute. Add lemon juice and cool. When cool, pour over fresh saskatoons in pie shell. Cook 1 hour at 350° F. Serve with whipped cream or ice cream.

Vanilla Buttermilk Pie

Evelyn Livingstone
Val Terra Herefords, Vermilion, Alberta

This is a creamy, flavorful pie that is delicious served warm or cold.

SERVES 6 TO 8

½ cup	butter
⅔ cup	sugar
3	eggs
3 tbsp	flour
½ tsp	salt
½ tsp	grated lemon rind
2 cups	buttermilk
2 tsp	vanilla
1	unbaked single-crust pie shell

❧ Cream butter and sugar until fluffy. Beat eggs, add flour and mix well. Stir in salt, lemon rind, buttermilk and vanilla. Pour mixture into pie shell and bake until knife inserted into center of pie comes out clean.

Raisin Pie Filling

This spicy pie filling provides a delicious dessert. Serve with vanilla ice cream.

MAKES 1 CUP

1 tbsp	cornstarch
1 cup	brown sugar
1 cup	boiling water
1 cup	raisins
½ tsp	ground nutmeg
	dash of ground cinnamon
1	unbaked double-crust pie shell

&. Mix cornstarch with brown sugar. Add boiling water and raisins. When thickened, remove from heat and add spices. Pour into pie crust. Place top crust over filling. Bake for 10 minutes at 400° F, then continue baking at 350° F for another 30 to 35 minutes.

Never-Fail Pie Crust

Peggy Herman
Herman's Horned Herefords, Bindloss, Alberta

Peggy makes this for brandings and family get-togethers. The dough can be frozen or kept in the refrigerator for several days.

MAKES ENOUGH FOR 3 PIES

1	egg, beaten
1 tbsp	vinegar
¾ cup	chilled water
5 cups	flour
1 tsp	baking powder
1 tbsp	brown sugar
1 lb	lard

🍂 Mix egg, vinegar and water and set aside. Sift flour, baking powder and sugar. Cut in lard and blend well. Add egg mixture and mix well.

Chocolate Sauce

Barbara Hughes
Chinook Ranch, Longview, Alberta

This is an easy dessert served with ice cream. Barb's mother-in-law always made this for her family and Barb now carries on the tradition.

SERVES 8 TO 10

½ cup	white or brown sugar
1 ½ cups	boiling water
6 tbsp	chocolate, grated
— or —	
⅓ cup	cocoa
1 ⅓ tbsp	cornstarch
½ cup	cold water
⅛ tsp	salt
½ tsp	vanilla

&. Make syrup by boiling sugar and water for 5 minutes. Mix chocolate or cocoa and cornstarch in cold water until smooth. Add to syrup mixture. Add salt and boil for three minutes, or until thick. Flavor with vanilla and serve hot over ice cream.

[Preserves]

Rhubarb Conserve

Patricia and Bill Dunn
Mosquito Creek Ranch, Cayley, Alberta

This recipe makes a not-too-sweet jam that is a favorite of anyone who likes rhubarb. Great on toast or with biscuits!

MAKES 12 CUPS

14 cups	rhubarb, cut in ½-inch pieces
6 to 7 cups	sugar
3 cups	raisins
2	oranges, juice and chopped rind

❧ Combine all ingredients in a heavy pot and let stand for 30 minutes, or until juice forms. Slowly bring to a boil and simmer, uncovered, stirring often, especially near the end. Simmer for about 45 minutes, or until mixture reaches jam-like consistency. Pour into hot, sterilized jars and seal. Once conserve has reached room temperature, store in a cool place.

Crabapple Butter

Don and Joyce Ulrich
Ulrich Polled Herefords, Medicine Hat, Alberta

Crabapple butter is an old pioneer recipe.

10 cups	crabapple pulp
9 cups	sugar
2 tsp	ground cinnamon
	juice from 1 lemon

❧ Remove stems and tails from crabapples and cook apples whole in a small amount of water until mushy. Mash through a strainer or colander.

❧ Place 10 cups pulp in a large jam kettle or pot. Add sugar, then bring almost to a boil, stirring constantly. Add cinnamon and lemon juice. Put in sterilized jars and seal with melted wax.

❧ Because of the natural pectin in the crabapples, the longer it cooks, the thicker the jam will become. Check its thickness by putting a small amount of jam on a saucer and let it cool. You may want to simmer the jam gently for a few minutes, making sure to stir constantly.

[Beverages]

Ranch Coffee

Mary Lou Grabowsky
Douglas Lake Ranch, Douglas Lake, British Columbia

Not only a working cattle ranch, Douglas Lake offers world-class stocked lakes for fee-fishery, public camping and cottages as well as horseback riding and ranch tours.

This coffee is a flavorful beverage that can be cooked on a conventional stove or over an open fire.

MAKES 8 CUPS

2 quarts	cold water
1 cup	ground coffee
8 tsp	egg, beaten
8 tsp	cold water
	dash salt
¼ cup	cold water

❧ Prepare egg by beating whole eggs. Keep in refrigerator or in a jar in creek.

❧ Heat water in a large pot. Mix 1 cup ground coffee with prepared egg, water and salt. When water boils, stir in coffee mixture. Return to a boil, stirring occasionally. Turn off heat and pour in ¼ cup water. Let stand 10 minutes.

Lemonade-Rhubarb Punch

Sally Hanson
Bell L Ranches, Airdrie, Alberta

A super summertime punch that takes advantage of rhubarb season.

SERVES 20 TO 24

7 to 8 cups	rhubarb
1	6 oz can pink lemonade concentrate
2	6 oz cans water
½ cup	sugar
1	2 quart bottle ginger ale

❧ Cook and drain rhubarb. Mix all ingredients together. Add ginger ale just before serving.

Cowboy Country Special Occasions

PROBABLY THE SINGLE THING IN LIFE THAT MOST warms a rancher's heart is the sight of cows grazing on a lush green hillside with baby calves frolicking nearby. But a close second would be the opportunity to socialize with one's friends and neighbors. Good food, good fellowship and the swapping of stories (some of which are awful close to being true) add up to a good time, Western-style!

Cowboy Country Breakfast

Trail Breakfast with Salsa
Bacon
Frypan Cornbread
Cowboy Coffee

This menu is for those times when you need to come up with a hearty breakfast on the trail. There's nothing like a clear, crisp morning with a crackling fire, the smell of freshly brewed coffee, the aroma of pine needles and sage and the sound of a stream or river rushing over rocks.

Cook this breakfast over the campfire using a large cast iron frying pan. Cook bacon first, reserving some of the pan drippings for salsa and cornbread recipes. Set bacon aside in a covered dish and keep warm.

SERVES 6 TO 8

Trail Breakfast with Salsa

8 cups	cooked potatoes, cubed
1 cup	green bell pepper, chopped
4 tbsp	onion, chopped
⅔ cup	butter
	salt and pepper to taste
1 tsp	chili powder
8	eggs
2 cups	sharp cheese, grated
	salsa (recipe next page)

❧ Fry potatoes, green pepper and onion in butter until lightly browned. Season with salt, pepper and chili powder.

❧ Break eggs over top. Cover and cook until eggs are almost cooked. Sprinkle with grated cheese. Cover just long enough to melt cheese. Serve with salsa.

Salsa

4 tbsp	onion, minced
4 tbsp	bacon drippings
2	small cloves garlic, minced
½ tsp	oregano
2	8 oz cans green chiles, chopped
2	28 oz cans tomatoes
2	sprigs cilantro, minced

❧ Wilt onion in bacon drippings. Add remaining ingredients and simmer for 30 minutes. Serve with trail breakfast.

Frypan Cornbread

1 cup	cornmeal
1 cup	flour
¼ cup	sugar
½ tsp	salt
4 tsp	baking powder
1	egg, beaten
1 cup	milk
¼ cup	shortening
	bacon drippings

❧ Combine dry ingredients. In a separate bowl, combine egg, milk and shortening. Add egg mixture to dry ingredients and mix well. Melt bacon drippings in a heavy cast iron frying pan. Pour cornbread batter into pan. Cover and cook over coals until done. Cut in wedges and serve.

Cowboy Coffee

1 ½ to 2 quarts	fresh water
5 to 6 heaping tbsp	coffee grounds

❧ Heat water in a large saucepan to boiling point. Add coffee. Boil several minutes. Set pot away from heat and allow grounds to settle. Serve.

Cowboy Country Picnic

Fried Chicken
Potato Salad
Green Salad
Johnnycake
Chocolate Layer Cake
Fresh Lemonade

Having the opportunity to eat in an outdoor setting is about as pleasurable an experience as any cowboy or cowgirl could want. The great thing about this menu is that all the dishes can be prepared ahead.

SERVES 6 TO 8

Fried Chicken

2	frying chickens, cut into pieces
	vegetable shortening for frying
	flour, salt and pepper
	seasoning salt (optional)
3 to 4	eggs, beaten

🐾 Heat shortening in two large frying pans. In a large bowl, combine flour, salt, pepper and seasoning salt. In another bowl, beat eggs. Dip chicken pieces in flour, then in egg. Fry until golden brown. As each piece of chicken is finished, place in a large roaster or casserole dish. Bake in a 325° F oven for about 1 hour, or until chicken is no longer pink.

Potato Salad

8 to 10	large potatoes
6 to 8	hard-boiled eggs
¼ cup	radishes, sliced
3 to 4	green onions, sliced
½ cup	celery, diced
	salt and pepper to taste
	sweet pickles, chopped (optional)
¼ tsp	dry mustard (optional)
½ to ¾ cup	salad dressing (recipe next page)
¾ to 1 cup	cream, whipped
	paprika

🐾 Cook potatoes and eggs. Reserve one egg for garnish. Cool, peel and cut potatoes and remaining eggs into cubes. Place in a large salad bowl. Add onions, radishes, celery and seasonings. Fold dressing into stiffly whipped cream and add to salad. Slice reserved egg and arrange on top as garnish. Sprinkle with paprika. Refrigerate until ready to serve.

Old-Fashioned Salad Dressing

Before commercial salad dressings came on the market, this old-fashioned recipe was used for potato and cabbage salads.

MAKES 2 CUPS

2 tbsp	flour
2 tbsp	sugar
1 tsp	salt
1 ½ tsp	dry mustard
1	egg, beaten
1 cup	milk
2 tbsp	butter
⅓ cup	cider vinegar

🍃 In a saucepan, combine flour, sugar, salt and mustard. Add egg. Slowly add milk and vinegar, stirring constantly until mixture is thick. Cool and use on your favorite salad.

Green Salad

2	heads leaf lettuce, torn into small pieces
3 to 4	green onions, chopped
5 to 6	radishes, sliced
2	stalks celery, diced
3 to 4	fresh tomatoes, chopped

½ to 1 cup	whipping cream
2 to 3 tbsp	vinegar
¼ cup	white sugar
	salt and pepper to taste

&. Tear lettuce and place in a large salad bowl. Chop remaining vegetables and add. Combine cream, vinegar, sugar, salt and pepper in a small jar with a lid. Shake well. Toss salad with dressing just before serving.

Johnnycake

In some regions cornbread is known as Johnnycake. This is a different kind of Johnnycake because it is slightly sweet and has a dusting of cinnamon on top. It tastes wonderful with fried chicken.

¾ cup	butter
1 cup	sugar
3	eggs
2 cups	flour
1 cup	cornmeal
3 tsp	baking powder
¼ tsp	salt
1 ¼ cups	milk
1 tsp	cinnamon

&. Cream butter and sugar. Add eggs one at a time and beat well. In a separate bowl, combine flour, cornmeal, baking powder and salt. Add alternately to the creamed mixture with milk.

&. Pour into a greased 8 x 8-inch baking pan. Sprinkle top of batter with cinnamon. The cinnamon will disappear as the cake bakes, but there will still be a hint of cinnamon flavor.

• Bake at 350° F for 30 minutes. Do not overbake. This is a very moist cake that is good cold or piping hot, dripping with butter.

Chocolate Layer Cake

1 ¾ cups	flour
1 ½ cups	sugar
½ cup	cocoa
1 tsp	baking powder
1 tsp	baking soda
1 tsp	salt
1 tsp	cinnamon
½ cup	butter
⅔ cup	sour milk or buttermilk
⅓ cup	strong coffee, cooled
2	eggs
1 tsp	vanilla

• Combine dry ingredients in a large mixing bowl. (Please note that sour milk may be made by combining 1 tablespoon vinegar with 1 cup milk.) Add softened butter, ⅓ cup sour milk and coffee. Beat until well blended. Add remaining sour milk, eggs and vanilla. Beat until smooth. Pour into two greased 8-inch layer cake pans. Bake at 350° F for 30 to 35 minutes, or until cake pulls slightly away from edges of pans and a toothpick inserted in center of cakes comes out clean. This cake is delicious with raspberry jam between the layers and a chocolate butter icing (recipe page 295) over top. Double icing recipe for this cake.

Fresh Lemonade

	juice from 6 lemons
1 cup	sugar or to taste
7 cups	cold water
	lemon slices, garnish

❧ Combine all ingredients in large pitcher and mix until sugar dissolves. Serve over crushed ice and garnish with lemon slices.

Cowboy Country Barbecue

Barbecued Steak
Mixed Vegetables in Foil
Corn on the Cob
Garlic Bread
Nanaimo Bars
Lemonade
Beer

It's a hot summer day, the chores are done and the smell of charcoal or mesquite hangs in the air. It's time to set up the lawn chairs, break out the refreshments and throw steaks on the grill. The nanaimo bars can be made well ahead of time. Chill the lemonade and beer so they're frosty cool when you're ready to eat. Then start cooking!

SERVES 6

Barbecued Steak

6	T-bone or rib steaks

— or —

3   large pieces of sirloin
            salt, pepper and garlic powder to taste
            barbecue sauce (optional)

૏ Season steaks with salt, pepper and garlic powder. Barbecue over hot coals. Baste with barbecue sauce, if desired.

Mixed Vegetables in Foil

6   potatoes, scrubbed clean and sliced
12   carrots, sliced
2   large onions, sliced
            salt and pepper to taste
            butter

૏ Divide vegetables between six foil pouches, making sure each pouch has all three vegetable and is seasoned with salt and pepper. Add 1 tablespoon of butter on top of each pile of vegetables. Seal ends of foil well. Bake vegetable pouches on grill or in 350° F oven for 1 to 1 ½ hours. Vegetables can also be layered in a casserole dish with salt, pepper and butter and baked in oven.

Corn on the Cob

6   sweet corn on cob
            large pot of boiling water
½ cup   sugar
            melted butter
            salt and pepper to taste

⋙ Remove husks and place corn in boiling water to which sugar has been added. Boil for 5 to 7 minutes, or until tender. Don't overboil. Remove, drain and let each guest dip their cob in a quart sealer or large jar that has been filled with warm melted butter. Salt and pepper to taste.

Garlic Bread

1	large loaf French bread
½ cup	butter
1	clove garlic, minced
	parsley

⋙ Cut bread into thick slices. Melt butter in a saucepan and sauté garlic until soft. Remove from heat and add parsley. Using a basting brush, coat both sides of each slice of bread with the butter-garlic mixture. Put loaf back together and wrap in foil. Grill on barbecue or bake in 350° F oven for about 30 minutes (15 minutes per side).

Nanaimo Bars

CRUST

½ cup	butter
¼ cup	sugar
5 tbsp	cocoa
1	egg, beaten
1 ¾ cup	graham wafer crumbs
1 cup	fine coconut
½ cup	walnuts, finely chopped

FILLING

1 cup	butter
6 tbsp	milk
4 tbsp	vanilla custard powder
4 cups	icing sugar

TOPPING

1 cup	milk chocolate or semisweet chocolate chips
2 to 3 tbsp	butter.

❧ To prepare crust, melt butter, sugar and cocoa in a saucepan. Add egg and stir until mixture thickens. Remove from heat and add crumbs, coconut and nuts. Press firmly into an ungreased 9 x 13-inch pan.

❧ To prepare filling, cream butter, milk, custard powder and icing sugar. Beat until light, then spread over crust.

❧ For topping, melt chips and butter over low heat. Cool slightly. Spread over top of filling. Chill until firm.

Cowboy Country Wedding

Barbecued Beef
Baked Potatoes
Caesar Salad
Peas with Small Onions
Buns
Raspberry Ribbon Dessert
Fruit Punch

It is possible to host a cowboy wedding reception and be the mother of the bride, too. All you have to do is organize and delegate.

A large charcoal barbecue with a rotisserie that cooks 80 to 90 pounds of beef will really help, and if your garden is producing properly, you should have a wheelbarrow load of romaine lettuce for the Caesar salad. That just leaves potatoes to wrap for roasting in the barbecue and buns and dessert to delegate. You will also need a large cream can to throw the baked potatoes into when they come off the barbecue. This will keep them hot while everyone attends the wedding and will be easy to transport to the reception. Just delegate someone to throw the potatoes in the back of a pickup along with the beef. In order to keep the beef hot after removing it from the barbecue, wrap it in foil and place in large picnic coolers. The beef and potatoes will keep for a good 2 hours and still be piping hot and tasty when everyone is ready to eat.

SERVES 100 OR MORE

Barbecued Beef

2	roast beef, top or bottom round, 25 lbs each

4	cloves garlic, slivered
	thyme
	seasoned salt
	pepper

❧ Heat charcoals in barbecue. Make sure there are enough coals to heat barbecue for at least 2 ½ hours. You may have to add a few more coals the last hour of cooking.

❧ Prepare roasts while coals are heating. Lay roasts on trays and stuff slivers of garlic into any little nooks you can find. Make little slits in meat if necessary. For a stronger garlic flavor use more cloves. Next, rub all sides of roast generously with thyme, seasoned salt and pepper. Allow to rest until coals are hot.

❧ Put roasts on rotisserie and place in barbecue. The barbecue will cool down considerably for a while when the meat is placed inside. Try to cook meat at about 325° F to 400° F. After 1 ½ hours, insert meat thermometer and continue cooking until it registers beef-rare.

❧ Remove roasts, which should be crispy-brown on the outside and rare inside, and wrap well in heavy foil. Place roasts in large picnic coolers where they will hold for several hours. The charcoal-barbecue flavor will intensify and rich juices will accumulate in the foil packages. The roasts will continue cooking because of the heat generating from them, so they will likely be done to medium when they are unwrapped and sliced. The entire cooking process will take about 2 ½ to 3 hours.

Baked Potatoes

🍂 There's no secret to preparing baked potatoes: just get some help to scrub and wrap them the day before the wedding. If you have a potato basket in your barbecue, throw potatoes in the basket during the last 1 ½ hours of cooking. If they are a little hard when you remove them, don't worry. They will continue cooking after placed in the cream can.

Caesar Salad

Prepare romaine lettuce the day before the wedding by washing and drying lettuce well and storing in large garbage bags in the refrigerator. It will take about one garbage bag of lettuce for 25 people. If there is any salad left, just serve it at the dance later along with leftover beef and buns.

30	heads romaine lettuce
10	packages croutons
4 to 5	containers Parmesan cheese
5	batches Caesar salad dressing (recipe below)

🍂 Toss torn romaine lettuce, croutons and Parmesan cheese with the dressing. Fantastic. Expect everyone to come back for seconds!

Caesar Salad Dressing

The secret to this salad dressing is to blend the raw egg until creamy. A blender or a food processor is a must. Just keep making batches and store in quart jars in the refrigerator until time to take to the reception.

2 cups	olive oil
8	large cloves garlic, crushed
4	eggs
1 cup	Parmesan cheese
½ cup	vinegar
8 tsp ea	sugar, lemon juice and Worcestershire sauce
4 dashes	Tabasco
½ tsp	salt
½ tsp	pepper
	chives, basil and parsley may be added

&. Blend first 3 ingredients in a blender or food processor, then add remaining ingredients. This dressing can be refrigerated for up to 2 weeks.

Peas with Small Onions

10	1 lb packages frozen peas with small onions
	water

&. Heat water to boiling. Cook vegetables at a boil for 4 to 5 minutes. Drain. Season with salt, pepper and butter.

Light-as-Air Buns

The mother of the groom has offered to make buns for the reception and the lunch after the dance? Bless her heart. Here's a recipe for light-as-air buns. Just keep making batches and throw them in the freezer until you have enough. This recipe makes 20 buns.

2 tbsp	yeast
2 tbsp	sugar

1 ½ cups	water
6 tbsp	oil
6 tbsp	sugar
2 tsp	salt
1 ½ cups	boiling water
2	eggs, beaten
6 ½ to 8 cups	flour

⁂ Dissolve yeast and sugar in water and set aside.

⁂ In a large bowl, combine oil, sugar and salt in boiling water. Cool to lukewarm. Add eggs, yeast mixture and 4 cups of flour. Beat well, then begin working in rest of flour while kneading dough on a floured surface. Use only enough flour to make a soft dough that is not sticky. The softer the dough, the lighter the buns.

⁂ Place in a large greased bowl and let rise for 1 hour, punching down every 15 minutes. After fourth punch, make dough into buns, place on a greased baking sheet and allow to rise for another hour. It is a good idea to cover the rising buns with plastic wrap so they don't dry out. Bake in a preheated 350° F oven for 12 minutes, or until slightly brown on top.

Raspberry Ribbon Dessert

This is a delightful dessert. The recipe serves 12, so make several batches for a large crowd.

Base

3 cups	graham wafer crumbs
2 tbsp	brown sugar

⅓ cup   melted butter

CREAM FILLING

8 oz   cream cheese
1 ½ cups   icing sugar
1 tsp   vanilla
2   packages whipped topping

RASPBERRY FILLING

2   small packages raspberry Jell-O
3 cups   boiling water
1   package frozen raspberries

❧ To make base, mix all ingredients together. Press half the mixture into 9 x 13-inch pan, reserving other half for topping.

❧ To make cream filling, blend cream cheese, icing sugar and vanilla. Fold into the whipped topping. Spread a small layer of the cream mixture over the chilled crumb base and reserve remainder. Cool in refrigerator.

❧ To make raspberry filling, dissolve Jell-O in boiling water and add frozen raspberries, stirring until raspberries are thawed and Jell-O is partially set.

❧ Pour raspberry filling over base, top with remaining cream mixture and sprinkle with remaining crumbs. Store, covered, in refrigerator until ready to serve. Cut into squares.

Fruit Punch

4   48 oz cans pineapple juice
2   6 oz cans frozen orange juice

	concentrate
2	6 oz cans frozen lemonade
	concentrate
4	2 quart bottles gingerale
	vodka (optional)

&. Mix juices together. Add gingerale just before serving. Vodka may be added, if desired.

Cowboy Country Christmas

Roast Turkey with Stuffing
Cranberry Sauce
Creamy Mashed Potato Bake
Sweet Potato Casserole
Brussel Sprouts
Buns
Holiday Fruit Salad
Mincemeat Pie
Steamed Pudding with Two Sauces
Old-Fashioned Egg Nog

Ranch people from the Rio Grande to the Mighty Peace tend to be traditional when it comes to celebrating the holiday season. It's a time of year that combines friendship and food, with family, neighbors and hired hands joining in the festivities. Here is a menu for Christmas Day that is reminiscent of what was on the table when Grandma was young.

SERVES 8 TO 10

Roast Turkey with Stuffing

1	12 pound turkey, washed and dried
10 cups	day-old bread, cubed
½ cup	butter
1	large onion, finely chopped
3	stalks celery, finely chopped
½ tsp	celery salt
1 tsp ea	salt, pepper, rosemary
2 tsp	sage
1	bay leaf
½ cup	raisins
½ cup	apple, chopped (optional)
	stock from giblets (optional)

ᨀ Cube bread. Melt butter in a small saucepan, then cook onion, celery and seasonings for 10 to 15 minutes. Remove bay leaf. Add raisins and apples. Pour mixture over cubed bread and stir to coat. Giblet stock may be added at this point, particularly if you prefer a more moist dressing.

ᨀ Lightly salt inside and outside of turkey and place stuffing inside. Do not pack too tightly. Excess stuffing can be put into neck cavity or baked separately in a small casserole dish.

ᨀ Place turkey, breast-side down, in roaster. Roast, uncovered, at 325° to 350° F for 2 to 3 hours, then cover and cook 1 ½ to 2 hours longer, or until meat is no longer pink.

Cranberry Sauce

1	package fresh or frozen cranberries

1 cup	sugar
1 cup	water

❧ Combine all ingredients in saucepan. Simmer on low heat for about 30 minutes, or until sauce begins to thicken. Chill and serve.

Sweet Potato Casserole

SERVES 4 TO 6

2 cups	sweet potatoes, cooked and mashed
2 tbsp	cream or milk
2 tbsp	melted butter
1 tsp	salt
¼ tsp	paprika
½ cup	brown sugar, packed
½ cup	butter
1 cup	pecan halves

❧ Mash potatoes with cream, melted butter, salt and paprika. Spread in a greased casserole dish.

❧ Make topping by heating brown sugar and butter over low heat, stirring until butter melts. Remove from heat immediately or topping will harden.

❧ Spread topping over mashed potatoes and cover with pecans. Casserole may be refrigerated at this point. When ready to eat, heat in a 350° F oven until bubbling hot, about 30 to 45 minutes.

Creamy Mashed Potato Bake

6 cups	potatoes, cooked and mashed
1 cup	cream cheese
1 cup	sour cream
2 tbsp	onion, finely grated
2 tbsp	butter
	parsley, salt and pepper to taste

❧ Mash potatoes, then add remaining ingredients. Mix with electric beater until very smooth. Place in a casserole dish and cook for about 45 minutes at 350° F. Serve hot. This dish can be made a day in advance, then heated in oven just before dinner is served.

Brussel Sprouts

4 cups	brussel sprouts
	butter, salt and pepper to taste

❧ Boil brussel sprouts for 15 minutes, or until tender. Drain and season with butter, salt and pepper.

Holiday Fruit Salad

1	14 oz can pineapple chunks, drained
1	14 oz can fruit cocktail, drained
1	10 oz can mandarin orange sections, drained
— or —	
2	fresh oranges, peeled and cubed
¾ cup	maraschino cherries, drained
1 cup	banana, cubed

2 cups	miniature marshmallows
2	eggs, beaten
2 tbsp	vinegar
2 tbsp	butter
4 tbsp	sugar
2 cups	whipping cream
	fresh fruit for garnish

❧ Combine all fruit except banana and chill. Combine beaten eggs, vinegar, butter and sugar in top of a double boiler. Cook until mixture thickens. Remove from heat and cool. Add banana and dressing to fruit and chill for 2 hours. Whip cream until stiff peaks form. Fold cream into fruit mixture. Garnish with fresh fruit and serve.

Mincemeat Pie

This old-fashioned recipe is traditionally served at Christmas.

Filling

4 cups	beef suet
4 cups	raisins
20 cups	apples, peeled and chopped
8 cups	currants
½ lb	dried mixed fruit
2 tbsp	mace
1 tbsp	salt
9 cups	brown sugar
3	lemons, chopped in food processor
3 tbsp	cinnamon
1 tbsp	allspice
2 pints	vinegar

| 4 cups | beef, cooked and ground |
| 1 | unbaked double-crust pie shell |

🍃 Mix all ingredients in a large saucepan and simmer 35 to 40 minutes. Put in sterilized jars and seal. Let ripen one week.

🍃 To make pies, fill bottom pie crust level full, top with pie crust and bake 30 minutes, or until crust is brown. Serve with ice cream.

Steamed Christmas Pudding with Two Sauces

SERVES 8

¾ cup	flour
½ tsp	baking powder
¾ tsp	salt
¾ tsp	cinnamon
¼ tsp	allspice
¾ cup	raisins
¾ cup	currants
⅓ cup	butter
⅓ cup	brown sugar
½ tsp	soda
1	egg, well beaten
¾ cup	raw carrot, grated
¾ cup	raw potato, grated
¾ cup	soft breadcrumbs

🍃 Sift together dry ingredients. Stir in raisins and currents and combine well to coat the fruit. Set aside.

ᴥ In a separate bowl, cream together butter and brown sugar. Combine soda and egg and gradually add to the creamed mixture. Stir in carrots, potato and breadcrumbs.

ᴥ Add fruit mixture and combine thoroughly. Turn batter into a well-greased 1 quart mold. Cover with foil, tying foil securely in place. Place bowl on metal ring or trivet in a large pot with 2 to 3 inches of water in bottom. Cover pot and steam pudding for 2 ½ hours, then uncover and place in a preheated 350° F oven for 10 minutes.

ᴥ To reheat, steam for 1 hour. Serve with one of the following sauces.

Brandy Sauce

2 tbsp	melted butter
2 cups	icing sugar
1	egg, beaten
½ cup	cream
2 tbsp	brandy (sherry may be substituted)

ᴥ Combine butter and sugar and add beaten egg. Set aside. Before using, whip cream, add brandy or sherry, then add the egg-sugar mixture. Serve spooned over steamed pudding.

Caramel Sauce

¾ cup	brown sugar
½ cup	white sugar
2 ½ cups	boiling water
3 tbsp	cornstarch

1 tsp	salt
⅓ cup	cold water
1 tsp	vanilla
1 tbsp	butter
2 tbsp	lemon juice (brandy may be substituted)

❧ Caramelize sugars by melting in a saucepan until they reach a brown-caramel color. Add boiling water and stir until smooth. In a separate bowl, mix cornstarch, salt and cold water to a smooth paste. Add slowly to sugar, stirring constantly. Cook about 20 minutes. Add vanilla, butter and lemon juice or brandy. Serve piping hot over steamed pudding.

Old-Fashioned Egg Nog

6	eggs, beaten
2 cups	milk
⅓ cup	sugar
¼ cup	rum (or milk)
1 tsp	vanilla
1 cup	whipping cream
2 tbsp	sugar
	ground nutmeg

❧ Combine eggs, milk and ⅓ cup sugar in a saucepan. Cook, stirring, over medium heat for 6 or 7 minutes, or until mixture coats a metal spoon. Remove from heat, chill in a sink or bowl filled with ice and continue to stir for 2 or 3 more minutes. Stir in rum or milk and vanilla. Chill, uncovered, for at least 3 hours. Just before serving, beat whipping cream. Add remaining sugar and beat until soft peaks form. Fold into egg mixture. Top each serving with a dusting of nutmeg.

Index